Eloquent, enjoyable and necessary, the essential guide to the purpose, writing. Leadership in all its form, ... democracy itself, begins here.

Allan Gyngell AO, President of the Australian Institute of International Affairs, founding executive director of the Lowy Institute and former senior international adviser to Prime Minister Paul Keating

I wish I had this book back in 1980 when I started! Lucinda Holdforth is a great speechwriter who wrote for me and has since gone on to work with many clients. She has now produced the essential handbook for anyone who has to stand before an audience and persuade.

The Hon. Kim Beazley AC, Governor of Western Australia and former Deputy Prime Minister of Australia

This book is for all those who love words and the power they have to change lives. *Leading Lines* will be an indispensable tool for CEOs and speechwriters of every kind; it is also, quite simply, a cracking read, attractive to anyone who likes a good story.

Tegan Bennett Daylight, writer, teacher and critic

A book for anyone who aspires to leadership. Holdforth draws on her formidable expertise and experience working with CEOs like me to deliver this practical guide to the creation of leadership speeches.

Geoff Dixon, CEO and Managing Director of Qantas, 2001–2008

With an elegant blend of logic, idealism, rigour, wit and a passionate belief in the power of language, Lucinda Holdforth has written a deeply humane book about the crucial relationship between good speeches and good leadership.

Leading Lines is for anyone who cares about making a better society: every artist and scientist, every teacher and student, every activist and up-and-coming young leader should read this book. Holdforth shows how taking charge of oratory and the public self – how believing in something, and expressing it beautifully – can help you rise to the top and make a difference.

Charlotte Wood, author of *The Natural Way of Things*

On a subject to which I have devoted my whole career, I have never read deeper wisdom than I encountered in this book. In a style both learned and personal, Holdforth teaches speakers and writers how to give their audiences the human connection they seek. I'm not only enlightened by this book, I'm moved by it.

David Murray, Editor and Publisher,
Vital Speeches of the Day magazine;
Executive Director, Professional Speechwriters Association

Farewell, dullard speeches. Here are thoughts, insights and erudition to give the most tedious speaker a tongue of honey.

Blanche d'Alpuget, biographer and novelist

This book captures, in Lucinda's trademark flowing and relatable tone, important elements that will enrich a speech and help connect the speechmaker with an audience. Owing to her deep professional insight and acute understanding of what makes a speech tick, Lucinda's views on speechwriting make her book indispensable reading.

John WH Denton AO, Secretary General of the
International Chamber of Commerce

Lucinda Holdforth is a Sydney-based speechwriter who, for 25 years, has been working with an A-list of Australian and international corporate, government and political clients. She teaches rhetoric and communications at the University of Sydney, and provides executive clinics on speechwriting for the corporate and public sector. She is the author of *True Pleasures: A Memoir of Women in Paris* (2004) and *Why Manners Matter* (2007).

Leading ng Lines

Lucinda Holdforth

HarperCollins*Publishers*

HarperCollins*Publishers*

First published in Australia in 2019
by HarperCollins*Publishers* Australia Pty Limited
ABN 36 009 913 517
harpercollins.com.au

HarperCollins*Publishers*
Level 13, 201 Elizabeth Street, Sydney NSW 2000, Australia
Unit D1, 63 Apollo Drive, Rosedale, Auckland 0632, New Zealand
A 53, Sector 57, Noida, UP, India
1 London Bridge Street, London, SE1 9GF, United Kingdom
Bay Adelaide Centre, East Tower, 22 Adelaide Street West, 41st floor, Toronto,
    Ontario M5H 4E3, Canada
195 Broadway, New York NY 10007, USA

A catalogue record for this book is available from the National Library of Australia

ISBN: 978 1 4607 5729 1 (paperback)
ISBN: 978 1 4607 1104 0 (ebook)

Cover design by Hazel Lam, HarperCollins Design Studio
Typeset in Sabon LT Std by Kelli Lonergan
Printed and bound in Australia by McPherson's Printing Group
The papers used by HarperCollins in the manufacture of this book are a natural, recyclable
product made from wood grown in sustainable plantation forests. The fibre source and
manufacturing processes meet recognised international environmental standards, and carry
certification.

To Syd

CONTENTS

Preface

People are afraid of public speaking for good reason. It is a dangerous act, and the speaker will be judged.

All speeches are about the future, even when they are about the past.

A speech is a cultural artefact, a message from its own time to the future.

A speech may have many contributors, but great speeches have a single, ringing voice.

You can have speeches without democracy, but you cannot have democracy without speeches.

A speech sums things up, and points the way forward. It is both a resolution and a provocation.

Great speeches are works of art and agents of history.

A speech is the anti-tweet. Every great speechwriter is an anti-spin-doctor.

Every great speech tells the truth.

A speechwriter is, first and foremost, a writer. And every writer writes to change the world.

Introduction

AS LONG AS WE HOPE for a better way to live, we will need words to show us the right direction and inspire us to take the journey. For those among us who aim to be leaders, mastering the power of speechmaking – the art and craft of persuasion – is more important than ever. If you want to be heard these days, it's not enough to have something to say, you'd better know how to say it too.

This book will show you how.

With 25 years' experience as a speechwriter for senior politicians and business people, I've learned from those at the pinnacle of leadership. I've worked either directly with, or close to, two prime ministers and numerous federal ministers. As communications coach in a global strategy consulting firm,

I saw the essential role of persuasive argument in formulating, gathering support for and implementing corporate strategy. I've collaborated with multi-millionaire entrepreneurs from fields as varied as logistics, sound technology and fast food, and discovered the charisma of the personal vision. Most importantly, for many years I have advised, and written speeches for, senior corporate leaders in Australia and beyond – chairs, directors, CEOs and senior executives in multi-million and billion-dollar corporations, including financial firms, banks, an airline, a telco, high-tech manufacturers, retailers and a media company, witnessing the dramatic forces, stresses and opportunities that shape their days.

What follows is a detailed guide for those who write speeches, those who give speeches, and those who wonder if – in an age when the American President communicates via tweets – speeches are still relevant at all. I explain what will work, what won't, and how to get the best speech out of the most unpromising circumstances. This advice will be backed up by dozens of real-life examples; quotations from famous and infamous speeches; and personal anecdotes from the halls of political power, the cliff edges of corporate crisis, and insights from modern life. I also draw upon creative-writing techniques for practical ways to bring more energy and beauty into speechmaking.

But this book is more than a speechwriting guide: it's also an unabashed defence of the art and virtue of speechwriting, and an argument for its vital importance to modern democracy. Like Aristotle, I see speechwriting as a tool, like a knife, that anyone can be taught how to use, and which can be wielded in ethical or unethical ways. The wrong speech can start a war, or destroy a company. The right speech can foster productive debate, enable peaceful resolutions, rally communities to action, ensure that good companies prosper, and bind diverse people together.

That's why those of us who care about democracy will defend the art of speechmaking vigorously. Now, more than ever before – with the rise of affordable global communications – opportunities for leadership are no longer reserved to those privileged few at the top. All over the world individuals are speaking up and making a difference. One singular voice can reverberate around the planet.

As we proceed, I will set out the strategic considerations and tactical options to help you make speeches that are true, credible, fresh and persuasive. There will be some overlaps and reiterations of key ideas as we consider speechmaking challenges from different angles, and analyse the lessons of diverse case studies. This is a book that can be read from front to back, or dipped into for specific advice.

The right words can be transformative. They can shake a heart. They can reimagine the world. The aim of this book is to help you find those words, and lead the way.

My speechwriting life

THE FIRST SPEECH that grabbed my attention was delivered by my father, at my sister's wedding, back in the late 1970s. With so many of our relatives coming to Sydney from rural New South Wales, the wedding took place in a small chapel centrally located near Circular Quay. The raucous party then adjourned to a fancy nearby hotel for a buffet meal.

After dinner, fortified by a few brandies, Dad rose to say a few words. A tall man, he stood nervously in front of the old-fashioned microphone with its long cable, and spent what seemed like an age trying and only partially succeeding in adjusting the height so it reached his mouth. When Dad finally started his speech, it seemed to have three or four beginnings, none of which led anywhere in particular. His heart was full of loving feelings, yet as I heard him ramble helplessly along, as I heard his voice crack and fade, it was clear he couldn't find a way to translate all those deep emotions into words. If there were ever a central point to his remarks, it never became clear.

The speech seemed to last forever but finally petered out in confusion. My sister smiled ruefully at our father's effort and we all applauded this decent man with his good heart. But somewhere in that moment, I knew I wanted to figure out how to do it right: how to find the words and the way that would carry life's deeper, riskier material safely and effectively into the public arena.

Like most people, I'd had some passing experience of speeches growing up. A Catholic childhood meant subjection to the weekly sermon: you could say that for the first 18 years of my life I was given a 10-minute speech every single Sunday morning. Remarkably, I cannot recall a single story or phrase or image from any of those priestly talks over many long years. Not one! When I think about it now, I can only envy the fantastic source material the priests had at their disposal: Mary, Joseph and the celibate marriage; friendship and the Judas betrayal; Jesus and serious God-the-Father issues.

I'm the perfect example of author Thomas Mann's observation that 'A writer is someone for whom writing is more difficult than it is for other people.' My parents were smart but not well educated: Dad was a butcher and Mum was a secretary. We didn't have a great many books in our house; we had no spare money at all; and we certainly had no connections with people in powerful places.

Mum and Dad made enormous sacrifices to send me to an upmarket Catholic girls' school, and there I plunged myself into books. I loved the way a fresh turn of phrase or a telling image or a potent story could shift something inside my mind. It almost felt physical – that little click in the brain when the kaleidoscope of perception dropped into a new pattern. It seemed a miracle to me that someone I had never met could not only share with me their unique version of life but also connect it intimately with my own experiences, and even influence my way of thinking. In turn I developed my own almost famished desperation to connect, to transmit the whole of any thought in such a way that it could be wholly understood – which, I would later discover, is the fundamental goal of every serious speechwriter.

My parents loved each other mightily, but late at night in the kitchen they had arguments so fierce that as a youngster I would climb out of bed and offer myself as mediator, interpreting each one's side and gamely attempting to translate their point of view to the other. Mum and Dad are still married 60 years later, so my efforts were either very successful or entirely unnecessary. But perhaps those experiences – and that passion for creating a clear and shared understanding – prompted me to aspire to diplomacy as a career. This was, after all, a profession founded entirely upon the art of peacefully correcting misunderstandings, negotiating acceptable solutions, and helping very different people come together to make collective progress.

It took me two attempts to join the Department of Foreign Affairs, but when I was finally recruited in 1987 I found I had an aptitude for foreign policy. I spent nearly 10 years moving around the circles of diplomacy, foreign and trade policy, and political power. I was posted as Third Secretary to Belgrade in the former Socialist Federal Republic of Yugoslavia; I spent two years in the International Division of the Department of Prime Minister and Cabinet; I worked for Australia's trade marketing bureau Austrade; and I was the founding director of one of the early government programs designed to promote Australia as a brand.

This broad Australian foreign affairs community was an ideal training ground for a young writer. Foreign policy is all about words. It's about records of conversation, *aides mémoires*, joint statements, declarations, conventions, treaties and covenants. And, of course, speeches. Every single one of those words matters. You can start an armed conflict with poor phrasing. War only happens when the words aren't working any more.

When I was sent on my first and, as it turned out, only diplomatic posting to Belgrade I discovered that the life of a successful diplomat requires certain personality traits that I don't have, such as an extrovert's tolerance for an endless succession of tepid social events. It seemed I wasn't cut out for the diplomatic side of diplomacy after all, and so I returned hastily to Canberra. I wanted to be at the centre of power: where the policy decisions were made and enacted, where the hard thinking, reading, and drafting of policy was done.

One of my most interesting work experiences was serving as the North Asia Adviser in the Department of the Prime

Minister and Cabinet, where, among other things, I was tasked with drafting briefing notes for Prime Minister Bob Hawke to use in his discussions with North Asian visitors.

Our prime minister was a busy man; he required no more than a one-page background note and a single page of suggested talking points. Despite slaving over my draft, I would see those two pages or so come back to me from my superiors covered in red pen. There might be several more iterations before it was done, and always you had to cut, cut, cut the extraneous stuff. A painful process, but that was where I learned about the contraction of wordy language, the intensification of key points, the elimination of minor topics, the elevation of tone, and the inclusion of more questions, conversational leads and spaciousness.

Most of all, I gradually understood that leaders speak differently from everyone else, including even their most senior deputies. The brief for a foreign minister, for example, followed a rather laborious template covering bilateral issues, then multilateral problems and finally global issues. It was necessarily niggly and detailed. In contrast, the prime minister – the leader – was all about the bigger picture: building relationships, defining areas of mutual interest, cutting through the undergrowth, clearing a pathway to the future. I learned that high-level simplicity is the language that leaders speak. The details could be worked out down the chain.

It was always a big day when I drove the short distance from my messy cubicle in the Prime Minister's Department up the hill to Parliament House and parked my old beige Honda Civic in the officials' parking area outside the Prime Minister's wing. It might be for a meeting with the head of China's CITIC Investment Group, or a Taiwanese shipping magnate, or the Japanese Trade Minister, or a Hong Kong democracy activist. I would walk quickly into Prime Minister Hawke's outer office, stow my bag under a desk, and hover uncertainly, pen and notebook in hand, until summoned into the Prime Minister's personal office, a large, sunny room decorated in golden woods and orange leather, serenely located adjacent to its private courtyard.

The popular image of Bob Hawke as an earthy, gregarious, sometimes adulterous character was quite different to the composed and concentrated individual I was always thrilled to behold at his large plain desk, with my briefing note before him.

'Good morning, Prime Minister,' I would say. Then I'd sit down on an orange chair in front of him and try to look calm.

He'd look up, smile at me briefly, and go back to reviewing my note. My eyes would roam with nervous excitement over the famous swirl of black–grey hair, the wide mouth, the flaring eyebrows and moist brown skin. With a large and shiny black pen he vehemently underlined any sentences or words that struck him as important. I shivered with each stroke of the pen upon my words and held myself ready for any clarifying questions he might ask.

Then he'd signal to his assistant – a mere twitch of a mighty eyebrow was enough – that he was ready for the guest to be brought into the office.

I watched the Prime Minister as he crossed the room, extending one tanned, gold-signet-ringed hand for a handshake, then covering his visitor's hand to make a double grip that was both warm and domineering. As he led his guest to a seat, I would scurry behind him to perch in an alcove, the button on my pen already pressed down for note-taking.

The Prime Minister's conversations always began with personal courtesies – how are the children, the golf game? The conversation then quickly opened out into broad questions, but the exchange was ultimately brought back to the notes on those two slim pages. Key Australian opinions and messages were carefully conveyed, because the Prime Minister's relaxed style belied serious and professional intent.

To me Prime Minister Hawke expressed leadership in everything from the self-satisfied way he smoothed his tie, to the photos on his desk of himself in the company of other world leaders, to the sober Earl Grey tea he drank with its austere sliver of lemon. At the end of the meeting I would wait until the guest departed, then the Prime Minister would raise an eyebrow and give me his lopsided grin. Time for me to exit. I would be talking about this day for weeks and months, but he would already be moving on to the next thing, and the one after that.

When the opportunity arose to write the first draft of a simple welcome speech for Prime Minister Hawke to deliver I jumped at the chance (more on this in Chapter 6). From then on I took every opportunity that came my way to write speeches. As it happens, many very smart people loathe writing speeches (indeed, almost as much as they dislike delivering them), so I didn't face a great deal of competition. I found myself moving around the bureaucracy in various advisory and speechwriting roles, rising to the role of speechwriter for the chair and the managing director of Austrade, whose jobs were to sell Australia to the world as an investment destination and business partner. At every step I learned something about the way leaders use language, and what works and what doesn't work in speeches.

In 1994, with much more experience behind me, I went to work for Finance Minister Kim Beazley as a political staffer and his primary speechwriter. There I gained a new level of understanding of the mechanics of power and the task of leadership by watching the political process from the inside. I went from writing about narrow foreign policy or trade issues to the big national picture, the state of the economy and the political choices that Australia faced. As Leader of the House, Beazley also managed the government's agenda in the House of Representatives, and I saw how speeches on the floor of the house formed – and were shaped by – a dynamic network of democratic processes propelling Australian parliamentary and political life.

A short time after the Howard Government victory in 1996 I changed course, quitting the foreign affairs community permanently, and heading back to Sydney to work in the strategy business of Andersen Consulting, which later became the consulting firm Accenture. My job was to teach management consultants how to communicate clearly to their clients. I'm not sure I always succeeded, but I certainly learned a great deal about modern business communications.

Eventually I struck out on my own and continued my career as a freelance speechwriter working for senior business leaders, including the heads of a big-four bank, a telecommunications giant, a defence contractor, an IT company, a global fast-moving consumer-goods business and a finance company.

My longest professional association throughout my career has been with Qantas, Australia's iconic airline. Because Qantas holds a unique place in Australian life, the issues publicly confronting the airline have always straddled an unusually wide spectrum, including national politics, Australian identity, advanced technology, commercial competition and industrial relations. I worked with the company (while also working with numerous other clients) from 2000 to 2008 as a freelancer, and was then employed for about seven years as in-house speechwriter. The dramatic developments faced by Qantas during that era included a private equity takeover bid; a mid-air emergency when the engine on a Qantas A380 caught fire; a major industrial confrontation concluding with a nation-stopping management lockout; a major challenge from a revitalised competitor, Virgin; ongoing financial troubles; tough management decisions; and a dramatic turnaround in performance. With public interest sky-high, speeches by Qantas chairs and management were always widely reported and scrutinised.

Today I still write speeches for private clients, and I also teach the art of speechwriting, both at university level and within governments and corporations. It's a joy for me to share my knowledge, hard won over many years.

Most of all, it's a wonder to me that in this age of distraction, we still choose to come together for a speech. Perhaps it is because there is some rough magic in the communal experience of listening, and a grace that comes with giving an individual the opportunity to speak their considered thoughts aloud in the welcoming presence of others. We come together to breathe in tandem, to experience our own responses and feelings alongside each other – and sometimes if we are lucky, and if the speaker speaks truly, in deep connection with each other. We come together like this because to speak freely and to listen attentively is to be human; to express a core human capacity and a central democratic freedom.

Like all speechwriters, I respect the possibilities of power, and I am fascinated by the way leaders – and leadership – work. Anyone who thinks there is always a gap between what leaders *say* and what they *do* doesn't understand the nature of leadership. For leaders, the words often *are* the deeds.

1

Why give a speech?

WHY GIVE A SPEECH? It's a fair question. The speech is fundamentally at odds with the character of our age. The speech is undeniably low-tech, visually uninteresting and unarguably protracted. There must be other, less stressful, less risky, less time-consuming ways to tell your story and win over all those demanding stakeholders. How about a media interview, or a press release, or emails to key clients? Or even just a tweet?

It is true that a good speech requires a lot of work. But it has many advantages as a mode of communication. By delivering a speech you take full control of the space and the moment. It is a chance to tell your story, the way you want to, without interruption. You can anticipate and forestall wilful misinterpretations; refute the doubters and the sceptics; provide a coherent and consistent form of words for staff to use in communications; create a unified understanding of your vision and strategy among all stakeholders; reveal your reasoning; convey something of your personal style; and lay out your vision.

Politicians and bureaucrats are well aware, but new business leaders can be surprised, that big debates tend to spring up in the process of drafting and editing a major speech. The process can reveal profoundly competing perceptions within the enterprise about its priorities, strategies and future. A draft speech, therefore, becomes a useful working document that can drive a resolution of these competing visions (if only temporarily).

No interview has the same status or authority as a speech – no magazine profile, or personal essay, or column, or media release. Which is why people in leadership roles are more likely to be remembered, and held to account, for their speeches than for any other communication they deliver. A speech is not just a portrait of a leader's mind at that particular moment in time; it also becomes an indelible part of their record.

To fully understand the power and potential of modern speechmaking, we must first look to the past, to the central role of speeches in all democratic societies since antiquity.

The rise, fall and rise of speeches

The first champions of speechmaking were the sophists. These travelling educators emerged in Syracuse, Sicily – then part of classical Greece – in the 5th century BCE, just as people were throwing off their local tyrants, developing the rule of law, and working towards greater democracy. The sophists taught the theory and practice of rhetoric, and any other knowledge that might be useful, to aspirational young men in an increasingly open world.

By the 4th century BCE, when the scientist and political philosopher Aristotle wrote his *Treatise on Rhetoric*, the first complete handbook on the subject, the city-state of Athens had transformed itself into the world's first democracy. The primary vehicle for persuasion in that society was the spoken word. In the courts, citizens were expected to represent themselves before their peers; in the assembly (what we would think of as a parliament), any citizen could speak; and all citizens were expected to participate in administration and war. Comparing Athenians with the peoples of other Greek city-states, their great 5th-century BCE leader Pericles said proudly:

> *A man who takes no part in public business some call a quiet man: we Athenians call him useless. Speech we do not regard as a hindrance to action, but as a necessary preliminary; other people are made bold by ignorance, timid by calculation; we can calculate and still be audacious.*

Aristotle's practical handbook on speechmaking was designed to assist all those who wished to participate to the full in this vibrant and 'audacious' Athenian democracy.

Today, even after all this time, making a speech in our modern democracies is just one person standing before a group, openly expressing his or her opinion, hoping to persuade an audience to a point of view or action or belief that has consequences within their community. A constant feature of the human experience.

The biggest developments affecting speeches in two millennia have not sprung from any changes in human nature but from technological changes like printing, reading glasses and voice-amplification technologies. Some might add that the advent of film, television and the internet have focused modern attention unduly on physical appearances, but the ancient Greeks were probably even more obsessed by physical beauty than we are.

In the 2nd century BCE, Rome overtook Greece as the powerhouse culture of the Mediterranean. Republican Rome was never an ultra-democracy like Athens. It was, however, a pluralist society with an elaborate legal system, checks and balances on power, and representative bodies for different classes of citizens. The Roman lawyer and politician Cicero, who lived in the 1st century BCE, became history's foremost writer on rhetoric, drawing together many works from the Greek world and providing his own commentaries. Cicero was not a democrat, but he was a tireless defender of Rome's republican constitution because he believed it protected Rome from revolution and tyranny. He shared Aristotle's belief that man is a social and political animal, and argued that there was an ethical connection between speaking well and being a good citizen who contributed to a better society. Cicero's ideal orator was also a man of civic action.

Cicero's life is almost as important as his writing to our understanding of the vital role of speeches in pluralist societies. Cicero achieved the heights of power and influence in the Roman Republic without the customary backing of family wealth or military might. He was a self-made man: a Roman outsider who made his way to the top through words, wit, argument, relentless political networking, deal-making and superb oratory. As consul, Cicero was the 'first man' in Rome and he also served as an effective administrator in western Sicily and later Cilicia (in modern Turkey).

What happened to Cicero demonstrates the risk to free speech and its advocates when democracy is in decline. He was killed in a political assassination demanded by Marc Antony and agreed to by the pragmatic Octavian (later Caesar Augustus) as a regrettable political necessity. The head that had spoken such eloquent words, and the hand which had penned such powerful ideas, were severed and pinned up on prominent display in the Forum – as if to disdain all that rhetoric represented, and to signal the death of Roman-style democracy and the rise of imperial government.

A quick survey of history tells us that rhetoric declines whenever democracy falters. Following the fall of Rome in 476 CE, the Middle Ages represented a thousand-year period when rhetoric disappeared as society's decision-making tool, made redundant by the rise of the arbitrary power of the feudal overlords and the overarching domination of the Church. This was a long period without public discourse, and with low levels of literacy, little social or physical mobility, and restricted education. With free speech circumscribed, rhetoric was relegated to dry educational theory, part of the *trivium* of logic, rhetoric and grammar.

The Renaissance saw the rediscovery of Cicero and other ancient texts; the rise of independent city-states in Italy; a new merchant culture; the printing press; and a renewed spirit of cultural humanism. In an increasingly secular world, philosophical speculation began to flourish, and while the *trivium* was retained as a teaching tool, it was progressively subsumed within a broader humanist education. Classical languages and the study of literature helped make the well-rounded man – and woman. In the 16th century, Queen Elizabeth I of England was a popular leader who read Aristotle and studied Cicero in their original languages and used rhetoric to shape and win public opinion. (We'll look at an example of Elizabeth's oratory in Chapter 4.)

By the 18th century, democratic impulses had at last regained their momentum. French intellectuals and revolutionaries looked to the vibrant rhetoric of the British Parliament for inspiration, as did the American colonists. Debates about democracy, sovereignty and empire provoked intense disputation, with the political theorist and activist Thomas Paine and Anglo-Irish parliamentarian Edmund Burke among the great communicators of that era.

This period also saw the first modern democratic revolution. The American Revolution was inaugurated by the Declaration of Independence of 1776 with perhaps the most rhetorical opening clause in history: 'We hold these truths to be self-evident ...'

The cheek of that line! Just because we 'hold' something to be true doesn't make it so, and it certainly doesn't make it self-evident. But America's Founding Fathers were determined to generate their own fresh reality through the power of words. And they largely succeeded.

Through the 19th century, popular demand for democracy spread and intensified. Big issues were at stake, like slavery, the vote for women, workers' rights, the impact of industrialisation and resistance to colonialism. This period saw the birth of the free press. Speakers' corners were set up in London, Sydney and elsewhere, providing platforms for all kinds of cranks, activists and visionaries. In the US, public speaking and debates formed a vital part of civic life, delivering entertainment and instruction.

The 20th century represented a historic high of achievement – possibly *the* highpoint of achievement – both for rhetoric and for democracy. Democratic societies fought fierce wars – both hot and cold – against Communism, Nazism and Fascism, with free speech one of democracy's essential weapons against the demagoguery of tyrants. Within democracies, debates raged and rhetoric soared over issues from civil rights to economic equity, and from racial equality to military interventions. In non-democratic societies, individuals risked their liberty and lives to argue for democratic freedoms, as in the fight for racial equality in South Africa and democracy in Eastern Europe. From the beginning to the end of the century, democracy not only survived the major threats against it, it also made enormous and unprecedented gains. As democracy scholar Marc Plattner noted in his 2016 essay 'Democracy in Decline', 'During the final quarter of the twentieth century, democracy experienced the most massive global expansion in history.'

It was a remarkable century. Indeed, it was a rhetorical century.

Certainly, there were many occasions when democracies failed to live up to their own best standards. Nevertheless, it was in the fight for democracy that rhetoric took flight – whether it was Churchill holding Britain together with little more than words until the US entered World War II, or Martin Luther King Jr creating a vision for the US based upon civil rights for African Americans. Rhetoric even played its part in the century's technological achievements. It was only because John F Kennedy said in 1962 at Rice University in Texas that 'We choose to go to the moon' that the US did just that, after much trial and heartache.

Like their classical forebears, and despite every technical and intellectual advance, 20th-century orators worked within the framework that Aristotle had identified so long before. They appealed to the mind and heart, social values and moral character; they delivered their speeches under the single or combined banners of political deliberation, ceremonial occasion and legal debate; they used language that was figurative, emotive, logical, factual and dramatic; they sought the right time, the right place and the right intellectual framework for their speeches in order to raise their chances of persuasive success. The language of the 20th century's great democratic achievements was the language theorised by classical rhetoric.

The late 20th and early 21st centuries have also been remarkable for the way the nature of democratic participation has expanded and evolved. During my own long career I have witnessed the emergence of new, non-elected leaders with tremendous overt or hidden political influence, for better or worse. The most significant of these have been corporate leaders.

The communicative corporation

As recently as the 1980s, corporate leaders kept a low profile, confined to the top floor, the executive wing and their exclusive clubs. Not any more. In our corporatised and globalised world, corporate leaders are recognised as major actors in our democracies and expected to account for themselves in public more than ever before.

And there are good reasons why. According to scholar Joseph Vogl in *The Ascendancy of Finance* (2017), around 1300 corporations today dominate 80 per cent of the global economy. These corporations tend to hold shares in each other, effectively creating a global bloc of corporations that form an economic super-entity. These supra-national power structures, Vogl explains, pose challenges to the nation-state's traditional role as the major decision-making unit. Meanwhile, ordinary citizens are not only the employees or customers or suppliers of these companies, but contribute portions of their salaries to the retirement funds that invest in these same corporations. That means many of us unavoidably have a stake in the health of this larger economy.

Our corporate leaders therefore have a manifest duty to be transparent about their choices. The idea of the corporation as a 'corporate global citizen' operating in a mode of 'corporate social responsibility and sustainability' is very widely accepted in theory nowadays, if not acted upon wholeheartedly in practice. Every major Australian company that I have worked with prepares an annual sustainability report either fully or partially in line with international standards. CEOs are now expected to present themselves at annual general meetings and account for their decisions to shareholders and the community.

At the same time, corporations have become more self-aware and sophisticated about the value inherent in intangible assets such as their 'brand', and more conscious of the role of their leader in protecting and promoting their brands, both retail and corporate. A strong brand protects a corporation through economic cycles, internal upheaval and unpredicted external crises, and is essential to retaining the loyalty of customers and staff. Branding is so important today that we are seeing more and more company leaders wading strategically (if cautiously, for there are risks involved) into debates about issues like marriage equality or the status of women, where they believe this will strengthen their corporate brand.

There's a relatively unacknowledged but very important influence on the rise and style of this communicative, rhetorical 20th-century corporation. The management consulting firm McKinsey & Company was established in 1936, but its global influence soared after World War II. According to business journalist Duff McDonald's 2013 book *The Firm: The Story of McKinsey and Its Secret Influence on American Business*, McKinsey:

> *... remapped the power structure within the White House; it guided post-war Europe through a massive corporate reorganization; it helped invent the bar code; it revolutionized business schools; it even created the idea of budgeting as a management tool. Above all, McKinsey consultants have helped companies and governments create and maintain many of the corporate behaviours that have shaped the world in which we live ... helped invent what we think of as American capitalism and spread it to every corner of the world.*

In its rise and spectacular success, McKinsey (or 'the 'Jesuits of Capitalism', as its consultants are sometimes described) developed a unique competitive advantage. It placed special emphasis on the quality of its communications, and pioneered a style of persuasion that was so successful it would be copied by other consulting firms and internalised and adopted by its many clients, from corporations to governments.

The architect of that persuasive style was Barbara Minto, and her eventual book on the subject was *The Pyramid Principle: Logic in Writing and Thinking* (1987). This was, broadly, a succinct form of business argument based on Aristotelian induction. The aim was to create an argument that was logical and comprehensive within a few short sentences.

The answer (usually a business recommendation) would come first, underpinned by the key reasons laid out inductively. Each of these reasons could then be expanded with more and more information at the client's request. Some clients would be persuaded by the high-level argument; others would wait to be convinced by the full underlying detail.

At a time when most management consultants had been taught at university to lay out the sequence of their thinking, building up bit by logical bit to an irrefutable conclusion and recommendation, McKinsey flipped the communicative order to put the recommendation first and then back it up with reasons. This pragmatic approach, while still intellectually rigorous, was far more succinct and useful to busy clients.

McKinsey's 'up or out' internal promotions policy meant that many consultants who were not on track to become partners would leave the firm and join their clients as strategy executives, bringing with them the communication practices they had learned. Others formed their own consulting firms and introduced the McKinsey communications model. It has continued to spread. When I went to work for Andersen Consulting in 1996, the New York office had brought in a former McKinsey communications manager who had personally worked with Barbara Minto to introduce the same style of communications. I conducted training courses based on that model in Australia and across Asia.

Rhetoric in public life

The 20th century was not just about the rise of the immensely powerful, increasingly communicative corporation. More and better-equipped advocacy groups have sprung up to monitor these corporations and their behaviour – ranging from shareholder activist associations to consumer groups to human rights and environmental organisations and more. These groups all use public persuasion as part of their armoury.

Democratic governments too are far more active in persuasion than they used to be. Public awareness campaigns about everything from vaccinations to safe driving are based on careful analysis of the barriers to behavioural change, and assessments of the most effective methods of motivating people to amend their ways for the broader social good. Often governments will use the largely emotive appeal and repetitive effect of advertising, but to be fully effective such campaigns must also be justified by reasoned rhetoric from the politicians and bureaucrats. Those in charge will need to bolster the advertising with argument, explaining to voters and parliaments the merits of the cause and the justification for the marketing and advertising spend.

The social sector has also grown enormously in size and significance in recent decades. Charitable organisations once operated primarily as modest delivery services – giving food, shelter, goods and funds to those most in need. Today, the social sector comprises a vast array of well-resourced enterprises, and many, if not most, also have a public advocacy role – whether it's for better policy on social services, aged care, child welfare or medical reform. Fundraising for good causes in a crowded market requires sophisticated persuasive skills, from raising money for children's hospitals to funding ovarian cancer research.

We are also seeing new leaders emerge from previously untapped and sometimes unlikely sources: individuals who demonstrate leadership across global communities through the low-cost power of the internet and social media. Following the massacre of 17 of their fellow students and staff by a lone gunman in February 2018, the students of Marjory Stoneman Douglas High School in Florida could have been yet another sad and quickly forgotten set of victims of gun violence in America. Instead they mounted a campaign based on impassioned speechmaking and backed up by social media with the #NeverAgain project, which has so far led to the million-person March for Our Lives assembly in Washington in March 2018 and an invigorated political focus on the gun problem.

The TED organisation started out as a program of primarily live events to encourage communication between geeky experts in technology, entertainment and design, but has evolved into a global online phenomenon. TED Talks have enabled global leaders in very specific fields to exert influence far more broadly. According to TED's own statistics, Ken Robinson's TED Talk on schools and creativity has been viewed 43 million times. Hans Rosling's TED Talk on the use of statistical information on global development issues has been viewed 11 million times. There's now a TED TV channel that sits alongside Stan and Netflix as a form of educational entertainment.

And it's not just TED. Indeed, speeches from many different quarters are now posted online: Nobel Prize lectures, academic lectures, corporate speeches and political addresses. Inspirational speeches are back in fashion too, much as they were in the 19th century, and commencement addresses by famous figures like the author J K Rowling are widely shared.

The other remarkable new avenue for rhetoric is the podcast, which has become a large and lucrative medium for entertainment and instruction, with lectures and speeches from writers, academics and others available on a global basis.

With so many speeches being delivered worldwide, it should come as no surprise that organised speechwriting associations have sprung up in recent years – for example, the US-based Professional Speechwriters Association established in 2013; the European Speechwriter Network established in 2012; and the UK Speechwriters Guild established in 2009. Regular conferences and symposiums bring together a new generation of speechwriters (or 'executive communicators' as they are sometimes called) who are charged with overseeing the rhetoric of institutions, from universities to corporations to government departments.

From festivals of 'ideas' and writing, to TED Talks, to a massive global and local speakers' circuit, the rebirth of public speaking has been phenomenal. Forums abound. From my experience as a practising speechwriter I can attest that that not a day goes by without a conference, festival or panel taking place. All this activity creates enormous opportunities for new leaders to influence our world.

The challenge for modern speechmaking

So at one level we can see a revitalising surge in rhetoric, underpinned by the rise and range of new democratic actors and global access to new communication technologies. But as we know, the situation is not altogether rosy, because we are now seeing a weakening of – and a reaction against – the democratic institutions and mindsets that make great rhetoric possible.

In the 21st century, democracy is no longer unquestionably on the rise. Indeed, our democratic institutions are faltering, confidence in governance and politicians is fading, and there is a general view that the level of public conversation is poor.

Today traditional democratic speechmaking – like traditional democratic leadership itself – is under a cloud. Traditional leaders in politics, business and civil society can no longer expect our automatic respect. Let's face it, they are barely accorded a presumption of innocence. We may be shocked to hear of the latest abuse of power, but sadly we are no longer surprised. We've seen too much and been too often disappointed.

Anyone who takes on a traditional leadership role in the modern world comes up against a wall of cynicism – legitimate cynicism. The record is all too telling – from politicians rorting their allowances, to corporations ripping off customers, to investors stacking their bank accounts through insider trading. And then there are the churches and charitable organisations with their horrific long-term cover-ups of child abuse. In Australia, the Royal Commission into Misconduct in the Banking, Superannuation and Financial Services Industry (known as the banking royal commission), which commenced in March 2018, has exposed what many suspected: instances of possible criminal misconduct alongside a widespread diminution of proper ethical standards at the highest levels of corporate Australian life.

Which is why leaders who are seen as representing the establishment can expect especially tough audiences these days. As soon as someone gets into a leadership position now, we don't listen to their words with open minds and hearts. We immediately suspect their motives.

It's not just the idea of leadership that's under strain. For the past 50 years citizenship has also taken a beating. Consumer capitalism has turned us all into expert global consumers, so that active citizenship has been replaced by passive consumption. 'I don't buy that!' we will cheerfully say about an argument we don't like. I can't imagine any leader today calling upon us, as John F Kennedy urged his fellow Americans in the 1960s, to ask what *we* could do for our country. Many people would be perplexed to be asked to do more than vote and pay their fair share of taxes.

But in recent times we've seen a new mood emerge. A new kind of citizenship activism has arisen, driven by a backlash against modern globalisation. The Occupy Movement, the vote for Brexit in the UK, the ascension of Donald Trump in the United States, and even the broader anti-immigration agenda across western societies can be understood in many ways, but arguably can all be seen as part of a larger push for national sovereignty, economic equality and the preservation of cultural identity in an increasingly homogenous consumerist world. This new citizenship agenda is magnified by the enormous perceived gaps between the elites who have 'won' and the rest who have 'lost' out of globalisation. Modern leaders – by definition, members of the elite – have squandered trust. Indeed, they can no longer assume all their audiences share with them even the basics of a world view.

And then we must take account of the modern constraints upon the very contents of speeches. Political correctness has been a disaster for plain speaking and public discourse. In the name of tolerance, we have become far less tolerant. On a spring day in 2016, the American author of the novel *We Need to Talk About Kevin*, Lionel Shriver, gave a speech at Australia's Brisbane Writers Festival in which she excoriated the impact of identity politics on our society. Shriver pointed first to the example of some college boys in Maine who were caught handing out sombreros at a tequila party. This act of 'ethnic stereotyping' led to a range of criticisms and sanctions against the young men for their crime of 'cultural appropriation'. Shriver claimed the virus had spread to sanctions on fiction because, she said, people who identified with particular ethnicities, nationalities, races, sexual and gender categories and classes of economic under-privilege and disability were 'encouraged to be possessive of their experience and to regard other people's attempts to participate in their lives and traditions, either actively or imaginatively, as a form of theft'. For a white middle-class writer like Shriver, this meant being barred from inventing a whole range of potential fictional characters for fear of being accused of cultural appropriation.

Now, few people on the planet are more articulate than Lionel Shriver. In her speech she argued with passion and power for the value of literary art that fearlessly enters into the experiences of others, and railed against 'the left's embrace of gotcha hypersensitivity' that 'inevitably invites backlash'. She suggested that Donald Trump appealed to people 'who had had it up to their eyeballs with being told what they can and cannot say. Pushing back against a mainstream culture of speak-no-evil suppression, they lash out in defiance, and then what they say is pretty appalling.'

The heightened cultural sensitivity identified by Shriver has led to what I think of as a kind of unofficial censorship in public discourse, which is so fierce that only those people who are very skilled at getting their language 'just so', like Lionel Shriver herself, feel confident and competent enough to express a contrary point of view. People who aren't particularly fluent, or feel unprepared to navigate the rocks and shoals of politically correct language, have become reluctant to speak for fear of criticism and complaint. Indeed, even Shriver's own combative but reasonably argued speech was met with outrage. Columnist Yassmin Abdel-Magied walked out on the speech, and wrote later in *The Guardian* newspaper that, 'It was a poisoned package wrapped up in arrogance and delivered with condescension.'

Our legal system doesn't help either. Australian defamation laws are unusually restrictive, which means, for example, that many women who, inspired by the #MeToo movement, might want to speak out about their experiences of sexual harassment, or worse, are legally constrained from doing so in ways that American women are not. Our copyright law is also antiquated and ambiguous. In the name of protecting artistic rights, for example, even some public speeches may be subject to restrictive copyright protection. How can we hope to change people's minds if we can't freely reproduce and debate their opinions? Unrestricted workplace confidentiality clauses and sweeping non-disclosure agreements – increasingly common in national life – have the same effect of providing real or imagined barriers to free speech. Silence becomes the easier option when lawyers and cheque books loom in the background.

And the final point to make here is that the power of contemporary speechmaking is threatened by the intense and aggressive egalitarianism of the modern age. Who are *you* to tell me what I should do or think? The very idea rankles. Expertise is no longer automatically respected as it once was. Why should *your* view on vaccinations or climate change be any better than *mine*? When anyone presumes to put forward their view – well founded or not – there seem to be dozens of instant counter-arguments on Twitter, comments pages, blog posts and talkback radio. Rational debate is overwhelmed by shouting. Even the expert will be tempted to withdraw, because defending your own soundly based opinion against an onslaught of ignorant abuse just feels like too much hard work.

These are trends that weaken our society, and more particularly our democratic capacity to debate ideas and make good decisions. The answer to rhetoric that we don't like, however, is usually not *less* rhetoric, it's *more* and *better* rhetoric. In my university seminars on rhetoric, students are astonished to find that our sometimes fierce but always fairly conducted arguments don't divide or offend, but actually open the door to new insights and sympathetic comradeship. They discover that practising free speech and open debate is a better way to live.

Above all, we must not succumb to despair, for there are some good reasons to be optimistic. The world is changing very rapidly, moving from hierarchies to networks, from power flowing down from the top to power flowing *around* the system. We may have less automatic respect for our elected and appointed leaders, but the yearning for leadership and fresh ideas is still very much there.

It may sound strange, but citizens in developed countries today, and in many other places too, are probably better able to have their say and be heard by a large audience via the internet and social media networks than at any time since the ultra-democracy of classical Greece.

It's true that anyone who takes on a position of public leadership or advocacy faces an environment that is hard and full of risk, and failure is not uncommon. Speeches are uniquely personal vehicles of communication, and when they go wrong the ramifications can rebound badly on the speaker. But I'm with US President Theodore Roosevelt. He gave a speech in 1910 that many would-be leaders should take heart from today, saying:

*It is not the critic who counts; not the man who points
out how the strong man stumbles, or where the doer of
deeds could have done them better. The credit belongs
to the man who is actually in the arena, whose face
is marred by dust and sweat and blood; who strives
valiantly; who errs, who comes short again and again,
because there is no effort without error and shortcoming;
but who does actually strive to do the deeds; who knows
great enthusiasms, the great devotions; who spends
himself in a worthy cause; who at the best knows in the
end the triumph of high achievement, and who at the
worst, if he fails, at least fails while daring greatly, so that
his place shall never be with those cold and timid souls
who neither know victory nor defeat.*

If you have the courage to get into the arena, the challenge is to make sure that your voice is one that people can trust, believe and be prepared to follow. You owe it to yourself to make sure your voice counts.

2

The role of the speechwriter

FROM TIME TO TIME, I am invited to talk about speechwriting and leadership communications to young executives studying for their masters in business administration. These are generally up-and-coming young men (yes, men) with a finance background. I can see straight away the scepticism in their eyes. To them I am an agent of that most wasteful of head-office activities, spin. I imagine I can see the bubble over their heads as they contemplate how much better they'll do than the present weak-kneed crop of CEOs who depend upon people like me, and the rapid savings they'll make as they lay waste to the communications-team head count.

At these events, someone always asks me: 'At the end of the day, isn't it the results that matter? Isn't it what companies *do* rather than what they *say* that counts?'

Yes, certainly. Impressive results are clear evidence of leadership acumen and management success. But in any modern organisation, good results cannot simply be ordained: they can't be summoned by the wave of a field marshal's baton. Results arise from human actions – from collective deliberation, planning and implementation. To move from strategy to results requires the effective mobilisation of human resources. And we mobilise people by inspiring them to act.

Here's a thought: motivation requires more than a paycheque. We humans will only offer our full measure of devotion in the service of a cause we believe in, and for people we admire and respect.

The numbers are essential; of course they are. But to achieve those numbers the leader must shape and communicate a strong overarching story that brings together all the people involved and unites them in a common purpose.

Which is where the speechwriter comes in.

Using a professional speechwriter: virtue or vice?

A friend once asked me a question so morally charged it has vexed thoughtful people all the way back to Plato in the 4th century BCE:

> *If even the guilty deserve their own barrister in a court of law, does everyone have a right to a speechwriter to represent them?*

Plato was opposed both to the idea of professional speechwriting and to the sophists who taught the craft. He was an Athenian aristocrat and anti-democrat who argued that the sophists were teaching people to use language for their own interests rather than in the service of the impartial search for truth. Manipulating language was immoral because it could allow the bad guy or the weaker argument to win. It was Plato who gave sophistry a bad name.

Thank heavens, then, for sensible Aristotle. Aristotle acknowledged Plato's point that, like many skills, rhetorical skill might be used for both good and ill. But on the whole, he believed, understanding how persuasion works enables people with good ideas to communicate their views more effectively, and that is surely of benefit to society.

In public policy terms, I too believe all society benefits when all sides of a debate are effectively presented to us. That's how we can judge the merits of the decisions we are asked to make. Say it's an environmental question. The locals are against the development; the council is for it; the state government is passionately pro; the federal government is divided, but probably against, yet has limited rights to intervene anyway. All sides have at least some justification for their position. So in my opinion, our society is far better off when we have a habit of quality advocacy and civil debate in our community.

I have certainly drafted speeches that were amended, or augmented, to introduce material that I didn't agree with. This can be very painful. But the reality is that no matter how much the speechwriter contributes to a speech, it belongs to the person who delivers it. They get the credit; they also take the blame. Each speech belongs to the speechmaker.

And there is a surprising collateral service a speechwriter may provide in the formulation of a speech. She may, for example, do the job that dozens of cross-functional working groups or strategy conferences failed to achieve. The speechwriter quietly noses around the business, finding its most interesting and articulate people, and encouraging them to share their views on key strategic issues well away from the threatening environment of the formal interdepartmental meeting. The speechwriter discovers the points of confluence and disagreement, sifts the evidence and writes up the report – which may or may not be the first draft of a speech. For the leader, it's rather like having their own private investigator.

I see speechwriting as a worthy profession. If the speech is an essential part of democracy (which it is), then the leader who gives thoughtful speeches is performing their own fine and necessary democratic role. And the speechwriter acts as an aid to the quality performance of that task. That's why those of us who are speechwriters can take pride in our role; why politicians and bureaucrats and CEOs should be glad to say they use our services; why it's a good thing to let the community know that this practice exists. Words should be taken seriously and used carefully in a democracy, not only by politicians but also by some of our most powerful non-elected citizens, our senior business leaders.

Which raises the question: can speechwriting really be virtuous if it is undertaken on behalf of people without virtue? I am not of the school that says a great leader should automatically be a nice guy; that simply defies the entire record of history. Many great leaders have been deeply flawed and even horrible individuals. I have certainly worked with people who I knew were only too capable of being unfair, unkind and self-serving. I have worked, at least briefly, for people I didn't like and even for people I wouldn't say I personally approved of (if I were the kind of person who thought in terms of personal disapproval).

But there is no way I would work for, let alone write for, any individual or company with whom I have a clash of core values. That puts cigarette companies out of the question, for example. I take the power of speeches seriously, and there can be no virtue in any speech promoting a business that sells a harmful product, largely to poor people. After all, even a defence barrister in a criminal case only has to raise a reasonable doubt – but a speechwriter is employed to win hearts and minds fully to a cause. I couldn't try to do that for a cause I did not believe in.

Speechwriting in Aaron Sorkin's *West Wing*: fiction versus reality

Every writer knows this: whether we plan to or not, we wind up writing the same book over and over again, trying to achieve that dream of perfection we started out with in the first place.

The cheesy romantic comedy *The American President*, for example, was Aaron Sorkin's youthful, popcorn prelude to his mature series about the nature of the American Presidency, *The West Wing*. They are all whip-smart in *The West Wing*. They talk fast, think fast and move fast. The camera tracks them walking and talking at top speed down the White House corridors, flinging great lines about like so much confetti. It's like the best kind of screwball comedy – screwball comedy on cocaine, if you like – which, if you go by Aaron Sorkin's frank admissions, it probably was, at least for a time. *The West Wing* not only idealised the powers of democratic persuasion and the notion of the sensible citizenry, it also popularised the speechwriter and the romance of the speechwriting process.

The West Wing is about the fictional US Democratic president Jed Bartlett and his inner circle. We follow the President and his advisers as they grapple with the demands of the presidency and the painful compromises that must be made in order to serve the national interest most effectively – while holding on to power. The head of communications and lead speechwriter is Toby Ziegler. Toby is morose, prickly, arrogant, romantic, cruel, idealistic and rash. He is the one who holds the President to the highest standard, chivvying him about not living up to the 'better angels of his nature'; it is a standard President Bartlett himself notes ruefully from time to time he cannot maintain. Sam Seaborn is Toby's deputy head of communications and sharp-tongued, wildly indiscreet, overly idealistic, often at variance (if not outright war) with his spin-doctor colleagues, very smart in certain ways and incredibly naïve in others, snooty, pedantic and magnificently wordy and self-aware.

In one of my favourite episodes, 'Galileo' (series 2, episode 9), a press-relations guy from NASA has written a draft speech for the President and is trying to stop Sam from completely rewriting it. He appeals to their common professional brotherhood.

'We're both writers, hey,' says the NASA bloke.

'That's only if you broaden the definition of writers to people who can spell,' says Sam, coolly.

How gratifying that moment was.

For Toby and Sam, the first impulse is to tell the truth as they see it – a habit I have noticed in all good speechwriters – which often gets them into trouble. Each of them has a deep knowledge of history and is concerned with the bigger picture of the President's long-term impact. It's Sam who notices that a prospective candidate for the Supreme Court is against the right to privacy, and foresees that privacy and surveillance will become a major social and political issue. It's Toby who worries about the legacy of the President and ultimately gets into hot water for acting on his own ethical beliefs.

There are several ways, however, in which Toby and Sam differ from real speechwriters, or at least from me – apart from the fact that they had Aaron Sorkin to write their speeches for them. Both are supremely articulate, especially Sam. Like many writers, I tend to flounder about in conversation, which is precisely why I like to write things down. Neither Toby nor Sam ever encountered an infuriating technical hitch that threw them into a last-minute panic, whereas I seem to have some calamitous effect on all phones, computers, and printers, particularly when under a tight deadline.

When I was writing for one particularly idiosyncratic and charming chair, nothing much would happen in relation to a looming speech until she would ring for a long conversation *at the last minute* in which she would lay out very clearly the structure, content and themes of the speech that I needed to have finalised and polished for her to deliver *the following day*. On one memorably stressful occasion, I was faxing the speech to her hotel in Perth as she was running out the door to deliver it. Naturally, the machine stopped working for a cruel 10 minutes.

Another difference: while you might see Toby or Sam looking a little bit agitated before President Bartlett gives a speech, or pacing around as he delivers it, they never ever look as though they are going to vomit with nerves, a situation that I have experienced many times. On the contrary, far from worrying about the quality of his own product, there is a hint that Toby is so coldly judgemental of his leader's performance – and so incapable of hiding it – that President Bartlett asks him to stay out of his line of sight when he speaks.

The West Wing not only made speeches and speechwriting and public service seem sexy, but also, in the most amazing case of wish fulfilment I have ever seen, it conjured up a real-life president – with the successor to Jed Bartlett, Mathew Santos, stepping out of the TV and into global public life as Senator Barack Obama. Later, the writers claimed they had been watching Obama's progress as they created the Santos character.

And then there was President Obama himself. The speeches he gave in the lead-up to winning the presidency reinvigorated belief in the power of oratory to make a difference. They also initiated a significant change in attitude to the profession of speechwriting. President Obama and his good-looking young speechwriter Jon Favreau made speechwriting appear both noble and cool. And President Obama was secure enough in his own eloquence to allow his speechwriter to receive genuine credit for his contribution.

It's a huge transformation, given that not very long ago the convention was to pretend that speechwriters didn't even exist. One of President Bill Clinton's speechwriters, Michael Waldeman, recorded in *POTUS Speaks* (2000) that before President Clinton delivered his first State of the Union Address following his re-election in 1998, Waldeman and a colleague slaved over every word. When it was well received, they were ecstatic. At the after-party, President Clinton came up to them and draped an arm around each. He introduced them to an old friend, 'This is Jonathon and this is Michael.'

The two speechwriters swelled with pride.

Then he added, 'They're the guys who typed my speech.'

Today – and I credit Aaron Sorkin for this – speechwriters have emerged from the closet. Certainly, my own long-time reticence about identifying myself publicly as a speechwriter has become an increasingly pointless delicacy, a throwback to an earlier age and earlier experiences.

Today, far from hiding their presence, corporate leaders are comfortable in saying they work with professional writers. The world has moved on. No corporate leader in their right mind tries to do everything; they don't have the time. So they get advice on how to raise capital or do business in Asia; how to restructure the company or plan their succession; how to change a government's mind or improve employee morale. A speechwriter is just another weapon in a very big leadership arsenal. So it is no shame to have someone help you with speeches. It is simple professionalism.

Thanks, Aaron.

A special relationship

There is no single way, or even preferred way, to conduct the unusual and delicate relationship between speechwriter and leader. The process can vary dramatically, depending on the circumstances, personality and style of each leader and each writer.

At the highest level, it works best when there is a deeply felt common cause and an intellectual compatibility. That's when we get those legendary partnerships between leaders and speechwriters such as John F Kennedy and Ted Sorensen, or Gough Whitlam and Graham Freudenberg. In such cases, the speechwriter transcends his or her stated role to become a true counsellor to the leader – another part of the leader's brain, the reflective part of the leader's mind.

But a successful speechwriting relationship doesn't necessarily depend upon that high degree of intimacy. Or, indeed, any. Consider Peggy Noonan's relationship with 'the great communicator' President Reagan. Noonan was the best of Ronald Reagan's speechwriters, but she didn't even meet the

President until she had been writing for him for months. One of the chapters in her memoir *What I Saw at the Revolution* (1990) is titled 'I First Saw Him as a Foot'.

Perhaps it would be truer to say that even though President Reagan didn't have a relationship with Peggy Noonan, *she* clearly had one with *him*. She *got* him. She understood who he was, what he valued and what he wanted to achieve in American life. She got him because she shared his values and knew how to express them in words even better than the President himself. (Like a lot of actors, Reagan didn't think writers mattered much; he thought it was all in the delivery.)

I have some insight into these experiences. In a few instances, I have worked directly and intimately with an individual speaker over many years. In such cases, it works because there is congruence between us – I don't mean necessarily friendship, but a strong working relationship built on mutual trust over time. It becomes very effective because there are shared memories, a shared language that we have developed over the entire enterprise, and much of the conversation about speeches moves into a kind of efficient shorthand. We have taught each other how to work together.

Invariably, however, the relationship is lopsided. To be someone's voice or persona is to take a major intrusive step into their privacy. It involves a close observation of the leader – thinking about them, even worrying about them and identifying with them to some extent.

Sometimes there is a particular role that the speechwriter needs to play in order to get the best results. She needs to have enough confidence to be unafraid to appear stupid – indeed, on occasion, to *be* stupid. I don't mind playing the fool if it creates a space for a bigger, more generous, more visionary conversation. That's not a sign of my humility; it's a sign of my self-belief. I also have to be ready to ask the unwelcome questions when something I am being told doesn't ring true, because that's a sure sign that it won't work in a speech.

Speechwriters are likely to have a curious intelligence, a great love of precise words, a passion for citizenship and history and an ambition for a better future. They may also share certain less desirable attributes: introversion, a self-selected outsider status, an absence of leadership qualities. I am not deferential, but I have no urge to manage other people (and no great skill at doing so, either). I respect the aspirations of people who want to be leaders and I take enormous satisfaction in helping the good ones.

A writer friend once asked me, in confident expectation of an affirmative response, 'Is it true that all CEOs are psychopaths?'

Absolutely not! Okay, maybe just a little bit. Many successful leaders, in my experience, do share certain characteristics: outsized optimism, higher than average energy levels, irrational self-belief, a capacity for dissimulation and extreme resilience. This means that many leaders recover much faster than others do from difficult events or blows to the ego. It also means they can quarantine stress, so that while those around them toss and turn at night, they get a decent few hours' sleep and return to the fray refreshed. Certainly, I see these attributes in both the men and women leaders I have worked with. But generalisations only go so far. The differences between these rare individuals are far more interesting than the commonalities.

The speechwriter particularly notices the physical manifestations of personality. I have worked for people who are uncomfortable in public because they feel too short or too tall. I have seen how they control their nerves, and how they betray them. I know where they breathe (or forget to) in a sentence; the nervous tics of their hands or eyebrows; how their skin changes colour, or their voice wavers or hoarsens when they are angry or nervous or embarrassed. I know which words they will stumble over and which words they will use too often. I know what they are proud of and what they fear. I know how they come down after an adrenalin rush. I know exactly how vain they are. Of course, in any enterprise just about everyone watches the leader closely for cues on how they should behave in their own role. It's in their interest to do so. But the speechwriter watches the leader for cues on how successfully *the leader* inhabits their role.

The leader is very often aware that I have this window into their private self, but not always. Even if they do know, it is due to understandable self-protection that they do not openly acknowledge this. Ego-preservation necessarily requires at least some downplaying of the speechwriter's role, as Clinton downplayed Waldeman's. After all, it must be awkward to realise just how much insight into your vulnerable self you have given this individual and, if it is a very effective relationship, how much intellectual influence you've handed over.

I have also worked successfully with leaders where our interactions have been heavily mediated through their chief of staff or senior communications adviser. Senior advisers like to stay intimately involved in the speechwriting process because they recognise its strategic significance. Sometimes they take a dominant role because they fear the leader might resolve to be a hero and collude with the speechwriter to express a genuine opinion that strays too far from the corporate line. Conversely, the adviser may want to work with the speechwriter to push a conservative leader out of his or her comfort zone into new and more progressive narrative territory. Or they may simply want to avoid a personality clash, judging that an unruly, questioning speechwriter is best kept away from an old-style hierarchical leader, in the interests of professional harmony.

Having been commissioned by a consultant, I once wrote speeches for the global CEO of a fast-moving consumer goods business whom I never met, and who never even knew I existed. It worked very well. Another time, I started writing for the CEO of a bank who developed an early dislike, not of my drafts, but of me. I might not have been deferential enough. I might have probed rather too hard in my questions. It might have been because I was a woman. Still, his team thought I was great, so they just kept me well away from the CEO, paid me quietly to write speech drafts, and never mentioned my name to him again. I wrote for him for several years through to his retirement.

Sometimes it is a problem of style. I have written speeches for CEOs who want well-crafted obscurantism. But it never works. I just can't do that. For me, that kind of writing is neither beautiful nor moral. And to be perfectly honest, I just don't have the particular skills required to write that way.

I once wrote a speech for the CEO of a financial services business facing regulatory issues. It was a lucid draft that his team rather liked (or at least, were polite about) but he did not. He got up and delivered one of his usual rather obscure, coded, jargon-filled speeches, and his team never came back to me again. It has to be said that his company continues to prosper without me. That's fine too.

And then there are those relationships where the leader and I regularly sat down peaceably together, just the two of us, shared ideas and worked out a plan, after which I went away and crafted words I felt proud of. Speechwriting is personal, which means it is human, which means it is a mystery.

3

The leadership lifecycle

SPEECHWRITING FOR BUSINESS PEOPLE is not at all like writing for politicians, who give speeches for a living and know the power of words.

Words do not have the same automatic positive associations for corporate types. They may perceive words as a subsidiary, even inferior, mode of communication. For them, it's often about the perfection of numbers and PowerPoint decks. Which is why business people can sometimes rise to the very top without ever understanding what words can do, and why words matter, and how words can make or break a leader. And that's why many speechwriters who move with high hopes from political to corporate speechwriting quickly come to feel disillusioned and deeply undervalued – because they are.

But it's not only words that business leaders don't know enough about. It's leadership itself. So many underestimate just how steep the step is from number two to number one. Becoming CEO of a major organisation is not like any other experience of going up the next rung on the career ladder. Even those who have already been named CEO, say, of a subordinate business within the enterprise, discover that becoming the head of a public company is qualitatively different. Having climbed that final rung, the new leader discovers that, instead of sitting back to enjoy the view, they have only the most precarious foothold on a windy mountain top, no further way up and a long, precipitous way down.

Many people with leadership aspirations expect that once they reach the top, they will encounter nothing less than a welcome and sufficient power to enact their long-thwarted will. But what they mostly find are limits on their capacity to act.

A new corporate leader has a huge and complex agenda for those critical early days. They have to get rid of the disgruntled internal candidates for the top job; integrate their own key people into the top team; and fire the favourites of their predecessor whose exit the new leader has long thought overdue. They are already worrying about their first half-year or full-year results, which seem to be coming up alarmingly fast, especially when they discover that the results will be slightly worse than expected. Yes, more people might court and flatter them, but they have the new problem of who to trust, whose advice to believe.

The new CEO is suddenly perceived by others as all-powerful, but they are living on borrowed time, there by the grace of the board of directors, and more effort than could ever be imagined is going to be spent on managing the relationship with the chair. Most of all, the new leader is wondering how to execute the ambitious agenda they probably oversold in order to win the top job in the first place.

When a politician ascends to the leadership of their political party, their automatic first act is to give a speech. Politicians know that persuasive communication lies at the core of the democratic system and of their own authority. CEOs, by contrast, too often see communication as an unpleasant addition to their job, rather than central to its execution. And they rarely understand what speeches are for. They don't believe that they need to say the same thing over and over again until it finally sinks in; they feel a great reluctance to take an argument public; they are fearful of offending anyone; and they desperately want to be liked. In short, they have a limited strategic sense of the speech and its uses. They see only the problems and not the benefits.

I don't deny that giving speeches can be highly stressful. I once met a long-retired corporate titan who had given many speeches over the course of a long career. We were having a discussion about speeches in modern life when he suddenly recalled the very first speech he gave as the new CEO of a major Australian company. Even then, he told me, he wasn't a novice. He was ready for the job and well prepared for the communications burden placed on a CEO. He already knew how to get the best out of any encounter with journalists. He understood the brand of the company inside out.

In his hands, this new CEO held a folder containing what was a fairly simple yet solid speech laying out his priorities for the business. He was sure that the content of the speech would raise no remotely difficult or awkward questions. So on that day of his first set-piece speech, he told me, he walked into the ballroom of a Sydney hotel for his lunchtime address to a business crowd feeling, with justification, pretty relaxed. That was until he saw the bank of TV cameras up the back of the room, with an unusually large contingent of camera operators and sound recordists fiddling with cords, and pointing their lenses at the stage on which he would shortly stand. Then he spotted the radio guys setting up their recorder mikes on the podium from which he would speak. And he saw the journalists at the media table taking out their notebooks, waiting to capture any slip-ups in question time.

The new leader observed the level of anticipation around the room, greater than it had ever been in his life. And even for this seasoned campaigner, a man fully equipped to take on the leadership role, the transition briefly became overwhelming. That was when, he told me, he quietly backed out of the room, found a secluded spot and wrote across the top of each page, in large capital letters: *STAY CALM. THIS IS NOT IMPORTANT.* Which he knew to be untrue.

Some CEOs only begin to realise what their role entails when the wave of speech invitations rolls in. They may have thought they were taken seriously before, but now they see what it really means to be in demand. Even if they have loads of experience in giving second-tier presentations, they now take on the task in a much more high-risk environment. The level of expectation and scrutiny has dramatically increased. They are now the voice, even the face, of their company. The media scrutinises; analysts write reports for investors; and employees dissect each line. It matters what they say, and how they say it, because new CEOs need to bring many people with them: staff, customers and clients, suppliers, investors, analysts, governments at all levels, trade unions, the key media and the broader community.

How to hold this task together? How to bring all the disparate groups and competing interests into some sort of workable alignment? Well, that's where the speech comes in. A key way to achieve this alignment is through a unifying narrative. All leaders – it doesn't matter whether they are in politics, business, civil society, sport or the arts – *all* leaders must tell stories. Because if the leader does not communicate their own version of the story, other people will make one up for them.

So the question is not *whether* to tell the story, but *how*. And while it is not the only means, by far the most efficient means – the tone-setter for all other communications – is the set-piece speech, that formal statement about the organisation's strategy, purpose, direction and achievements.

There's another issue to be taken into account here. I see many leaders who dutifully repeat the same old speech over the weeks, months and years, without any insight into the critical role that the passage of time plays in any leader's tenure. Every leader's term in office will have its predictable phases and seasons. Understanding where you are in your own leadership lifecycle will ensure your speeches are always potent and relevant, serving both your reputation and your cause.

Seasons of leadership

Politicians (the good ones, anyway) have a very clear sense of the leadership lifecycle and how it works. They know from long democratic electoral experience what is required of them at each point along the way: the pre-selection, the election, the cabinet reshuffle, the valedictory. It's an established process, with relatively clear speaking requirements at each point in the cycle.

So let's think specifically about the CEO lifecycle, and the role the speechwriter might play in making the most of it. They don't have long: most CEOs can expect to enjoy a mere three to five years in office. Three years! A guinea pig will live longer, or a fish. With so little time to make a difference, a new CEO needs to understand – quickly – the tides and rhythms of his or her tenure, and map out a program accordingly. The speechwriter can help.

The honeymoon

There is usually a delightful honeymoon at the outset of a new CEO's sojourn in the top office, and in the glow of all that media and staff goodwill there will be a big temptation to offer a feel-good, promise-everything version of leadership in the early speeches. But the speechwriter must urge a judicious balance between inspirational hope and cold realism, between continuity with the past and change for the future. Any tough measures should ideally be signalled as early as possible, which may cut short the honeymoon but will undoubtedly strengthen the newcomer's leadership credentials over time.

The leader's agenda needs to be put in the context of a clear, big-picture strategy, and that is best expressed in a speech. It doesn't need to be overly detailed – in fact, it *should not* be too detailed, because that might box the leader in – but it does need to make clear the key goals the leader aims to achieve, their broad approach to achieving them, and the values that will guide their decision-making along the way. All strategy statements should include a reference to the importance of flexibility, just in case, as so often happens, all these best-laid plans go awry.

The very process of developing this initial strategy speech is a useful discipline for a new leader and merits close attention. What seems quite brilliant as it swirls around the mind – or is said in the job interview – often turns to mud and sludge as it lands in cold hard prose on the page. It is only in purposeful articulation that the weaknesses or deficiencies of a concept become apparent and can therefore be addressed.

One new CEO I wrote for insisted upon boldly optimistic initial speeches, boasting to his early audiences that he would completely regenerate the company through the transformative use of technology. Two years later, he demanded that all those speeches be taken 'off the internet' because the results were falling sadly short of his overblown promises.

The tough middle period

After the honeymoon comes the slog, and sometimes the letdown, of corporate life. I worked with one CEO who was shocked when the media turned on him about 18 months into his tenure. Pointless to remind him that this is what the media always does, and that he should just get on with it, trusting that the approval would return. He felt burned, and was inclined to retreat from giving speeches, preferring to shelter within his grand office on the top floor, where everyone was nice to him. He had to be persuaded that continuing to explain his strategy clearly and without defensiveness in the public arena would, over time, win back his supporters and earn him even more respect. And that to step back abruptly would be noticed and remarked upon, and not in a good way.

The middle period of leadership is marked by the seasons and rituals of CEO life. There are the obligatory reporting events like annual general meetings and half-year and full-year results that represent the framework dates on the annual calendar. These reporting sessions become opportunities to reinforce strategic priorities. They draw the trajectory between yesterday's decisions, today's results and tomorrow's goals.

This is often the period when the speechwriter really earns her keep. Because some things will certainly go wrong, even if they don't go fully to hell. That major project won't get regulatory permission. The currency will move in the wrong direction. Wage costs will blow out. The new product line will fail to sell. Whatever happens, the speechwriter needs to help the leader reshape the narrative – explaining what has changed and why, and how it will be managed.

Then is when apparent – if not actual – coherence and consistency are vital. The speechwriter may well be the only person in the organisation with the whole narrative in her head. So changes need to be explained within a long-term framework that respects the history of the brand and the business and resets the path to the future – consistent with the leader's broad vision. Change is put within the context of continuity.

Even within their short lifecycle, nearly every CEO I have known goes through at least one slump. It's a weary business, being the leader. The challenge is to keep up the discipline and routine during those inevitable periods when the heart isn't fully engaged. The speechwriter who has input into the CEO's diary can help, by accepting invitations or even devising events that reflect (or broaden) the CEO's profile. These might include charity events, employee functions or corporate anniversaries.

On such occasions the CEO will be asked to deliver a ceremonial speech; the low-risk address which does not offer new information or direction, but mirrors the values of the audience and invokes the spirit of the enterprise. Ceremonial speeches can be powerful opportunities to show the leader's humanity, and in the tough middle period they can remind the leader of the higher purpose that fired their ambitions in the first place. (I explain how to capture the full potential of the ceremonial address in Chapter 5.)

I have also seen the internal dynamics of a company, and the CEO's mood, improve significantly when an area of the business hitherto neglected – the environmental agenda, say, or the role of women, or new technologies, or the new service culture, or fledgling Asian projects – is picked up as a major subject of a CEO speech (or series of speeches). Even as the drafting process is underway, the status of those activities, and the people who undertake them within the business, is elevated. This influences forward strategy, generates internal enthusiasm, and establishes the CEO in a more mature phase of their leadership.

Valedictories

Which brings us to the valedictory period, those final months in high office.

For leaders looking to extend their careers, this will be the time for a calculated reshaping of their public image. Canny CEOs, mindful of their moth-like mortality, will seek to use targeted occasions to discreetly promote themselves for the next position. They might be looking for another CEO role, a place on the director circuit, or a prestigious public sector appointment. The speechwriter can help the leader reach this objective through speeches that round out the leader's profile. By making thoughtful public remarks on relevant social or economic issues, the smart CEO asserts their readiness for the next role.

Some outgoing leaders, however, will not be hungry for another high-flying, high-paying role. These CEOs will have a rather different agenda. For them, this may be the opportunity for a final artistic blossoming, the late period when all that accumulated wisdom, experience and knowledge can be put to best use. As they exit from public life, this is the time for the CEO to be brave, to be a good citizen, to say the things they were unwilling to say when trying to win and hold on to friends – or avoid annoying the board.

Most of all, this late period is the time, not so much to list the CEO's achievements, but to define the terms by which their particular leadership tenure should be measured, and therefore, naturally, judged by history to have been a resounding success under challenging circumstances.

The life of a CEO is, in many ways, nasty, brutish and relatively short. It's also lucrative and privileged, and creates an unparalleled opportunity to make change. Understanding the leadership lifecycle can ensure that this precious opportunity to lead is not wasted.

Learning (even more) from Steve Jobs

The most celebrated corporate speechmaker of modern times was – and despite his death in 2011, still is – Steve Jobs, the founder of Apple. Steve Jobs didn't sound like your usual business leader, droning on about cost cutting or growing profits. He spoke of ultimate experiences and creative ecstasy. He was rather like the Oracle of Delphi, and when he said his famous 'One more thing ...', you knew he had a hotline to the future. He was about to make an announcement that would rock our world.

Many CEOs would love to emulate the performance style Jobs pioneered: to present to passionate stadium audiences, with huge screens, vivid graphics and live demos of thrilling new products. Let's face it, though, it's hard to emulate Steve Jobs unless you are the founding genius of a world-leading tech company. I don't think too many investors expect retail bankers to spruik their home-loan innovations to cheering audiences, or mining executives to slink across a big stage in T-shirts and head-sets, marvelling at their company's new autonomous iron ore-train software.

There are, however, some useful lessons for less exalted leaders in Steve Jobs's approach to communications. Jobs is a vivid example of a leader successfully navigating the dramatic troughs as well as the extravagant peaks of the leadership lifecycle. He famously started Apple in his dad's garage in 1976 and achieved his honeymoon high in 1980 when Apple went public. At that point Jobs was suddenly worth hundreds of millions of dollars. Five years later and the middle period was going so badly that Jobs was sacked from his own company. By the time he was invited back to Apple in 1996, Jobs had learned that leadership is not some perennial honeymoon, but demands pragmatism and painful decisions. Jobs moved quickly to cut back unprofitable product lines, getting rid of the Newton message pad and Apple-made printers, even though there were as yet no profitable products to replace them.

One of Jobs's most challenging presentations took place in 1997. The audience was on a high; thrilled that the hero had come back to save the company and regain its pride. They welcomed Job with raucous applause.

But instead of making a crowd-pleasing speech, Jobs was forced to deliver hard news. In an act that probably felt like treason for Apple followers, Jobs declared a truce with arch-rival Microsoft. In fact, it was more than a truce: it was a massive bailout of Apple by Bill Gates. This move may have been essential to the survival of the company, but when the giant screen flashed up a giant image of the unloved Bill, all the Apple devotees groaned.

Jobs didn't get flustered. Nor did he back down. Instead, he gave a middle period speech, carefully reasoned and plainly facing the facts:

> *If we want to move forward, see Apple healthy and prospering again, we have to let go of a few things here. We have to let go of this notion that for Apple to win, Microsoft has to lose.*

Here is Steve Jobs, not as the heroic master of Apple, but its loyal servant, who understands it best, and cares about it most, and is ready to do the hard thinking and deliver the sobering messages required for its survival.

But importantly, that's not the only message that Jobs sent to his followers. If all Jobs could think of to do was offer a purely businesslike solution to Apple's problems, then he was risking the very thing that made Apple great: it's commitment to perfection over profits. That would have been very bad for Steve Jobs as leader, and probably bad for the Apple brand too.

Steve Jobs solved this problem by a fabulous rhetorical gesture. For in that same speech he declared that Apple was prepared to lose customers in order to preserve its integrity.

You still have to think differently to buy an Apple computer. The people that do buy them do think differently and they are the creative spirits in this world and they are the people that are not just out to get a job done, they are out to change the world ... and we make tools for those kinds of people.

Not many leaders have the outsize confidence to say something like this. Jobs made it clear that if you weren't eager to sign on to the 'Think Different' mantra of Apple, then he wasn't going to try and draft you in. He understood the immense psychic power of summoning the elect few to the higher cause – the few who would be prepared to pay a premium for the privilege. Naturally, we all couldn't wait to rush in and prove how different we were. As the iPod, iPhone and iPad eventually rolled out under Jobs's leadership, Apple went on to become the world's most valuable company.

By the time Jobs gave his Stanford University Commencement address in 2005, he was able to deliver one of the great valedictory messages, a ceremonial speech ripe with meaning and immensely fulfilling for the audience.

He started the speech by saying, in a deceptively casual way, that he was just going to tell a few stories:

Today I want to tell you three stories from my life. That's it. No big deal. Just three stories.

The stories concerned the time he dropped out of school but studied calligraphy; when he was sacked from Apple but started Pixar and a family; and how he was now using his approaching death as a spur to do great things. But in fact, those three casual stories delineated a clear and powerful structure: Beginning, Growing, and Ending.

The speech allowed Steve Jobs to reshape his image for posterity, converting his life into a parable of one man's quest for final enlightenment.

Most CEOs who worship Steve Jobs – and there are many of them – may never be able to replicate his extraordinary career or electric stage presence. But they can follow Jobs's lead and give their speeches the care they deserve; attune their speeches to the seasons of their own leadership lifecycle; and strike the delicate balance between continuity and change that characterises great leaders and leadership.

4

Strategic positioning

SO LET US NOW turn to the process of speechmaking in more detail, working through the stages that will take us from that fearsome blank page to a full and satisfying draft. In this chapter we will look at the strategic questions that confront modern speechmakers, including what to do with that elephant in the room; deciding on the real job of your speech; choosing the right vantage point; selecting your key audience; and building your reputation through the quality of your argument.

Getting the best from your speechwriter

First, some thoughts on making the most of your speechwriter. There are many memoirs written by speechwriters, and you would be forgiven for assuming that those memoirs would provide helpful insights into how to conduct the speechwriter–client relationship. But most of them are, in fact, laments over *totally failed* speechwriting relationships. Nearly all of them relate to political speechwriters and their clients, rather than leaders and speeches in corporate environments or more broadly.

The way these narratives tend to unfold is that the speechwriter starts with high ideals and big political ambitions, but disillusion slowly (or quickly) kicks in as their political client fails to live up to the speechwriter's hopes. The failure of the relationship seems inevitable. The speechwriter too often combines intellectual arrogance with political naïveté, and the politician doesn't know how to manage their speechwriter effectively. These memoirs make for good drama, but depressing reading. And it doesn't have to be like this.

As a speechwriter I've learned a great deal about the unique dimensions of the relationship between speechwriter and client. I have found that I often need to help my clients understand exactly what I can do for them, and how they, in turn, can help me do my best work on their behalf. So to anyone contemplating working with a speechwriter, allow me to respectfully make the following points:

· Your speechwriter is your number-one fan. She will also be your most severe critic. This paradox is precisely why she will do a great job. Only by recognising your flaws and weaknesses, only by understanding the deepest doubts and objections you will find in your audiences, then believing beyond all reason that you can overcome those problems, can she find the words to help you triumph in public conversation. It can make her a pain in meetings. But don't take offence. It's why she's good at her job.

· Don't spin the speechwriter. On the contrary, bring your speechwriter to the top table and help her understand the real story. The more deeply your speechwriter understands your true circumstances – warts and all – the better the speeches she writes will be. She's a professional. She knows how to tell the truth – even the unpalatable truth – in a way that not only protects your interests but also actively advances your cause (unless you are engaged in criminal activity, in which case you are on your own).

· Your speechwriter is, quite frankly, a rather fragile individual. She may be arrogant enough to write herself into the role of the leader, but she will also be self-aware enough to know that she doesn't have a leadership bone in her body, probably due to introversion and anxiety issues. In his portrait of US presidential speechwriters, *White House Ghosts* (2008), Robert Schlesinger depicts a litany of speechwriterly morbidities, including ulcers, boils, alcoholism, heart attacks, pneumonia, eyestrain, gall stones and plain old emotional burnout. I know of no serious speechwriter who isn't, as Ronald Reagan's speechwriter Peggy Noonan put it, 'pale and nervous'. Try to be kind.

· Your speechwriter is an incredibly hardworking and dedicated member of your team. It just won't look that way. When she's in the café down the road, or has her feet up on the desk with her eyes gently closed, or stares absently out to some imaginary sea during team meetings, that means she's thinking. As far as a speechwriter is concerned, thinking equals working. Behind that vacant expression, a paragraph is brewing.

· As the senior writer in any business, your speechwriter is also what author Saul Bellow once called your 'first-class noticer', particularly alert to any shifts in the world or your enterprise that will affect your narrative, for better or worse. Your speechwriter is perhaps better placed than anyone else to look at the longer-term picture. She is not just your wordsmith, she is also your 'idea-smith'. Let her frame your actions within the bigger picture (economic, commercial, ethical, social) to convey your vision and purpose.

· Don't just take the speechwriter's first draft and assume that's the best she can do. Or even that that's where she thinks the speech should end up. The first draft is a true set of initial suggestions by the speechwriter – a trial, an attempt. Sometimes it will go wildly too far and overshoot its brief; on other occasions it may be far too weak and timid. Perhaps it will still only circle the key point. That's okay; it's what first drafts are for. It doesn't

mean the speechwriter has no idea – it means she is
hunting for the core of the argument. Great speeches are
the product of serious collaboration between the speaker
and the speechwriter. Now is the time for you to knuckle
down, together.

· The speechwriter is not necessarily the right person
  to take along to the delivery of your jointly prepared
  speech. Don't be surprised if, on that occasion, your
  speechwriter fails to put on the mask of calm confidence
  required of all staffers in public, and instead looks green
  and sickly. This is not because she doesn't believe in
  you, it's because she is worried that she has left in some
  catastrophic blooper that will only be discovered as you
  read the text aloud to a worldwide audience.

· Your speechwriter will be more ambitious for you as a
  legendary leader than anyone else in your enterprise.
  And perhaps even more ambitious for you than you
  are. This may well be a source of tension between you
  at times. You are just trying to get along; she is urging
  you to greatness. You can use your speechwriter as your
  conscience, and your inspiration.

· Speechwriters, like all writers, are loners by instinct.
  This can make life tricky because modern speechwriting
  is in part a collective endeavour. In a corporate
  environment, for example, many people have to buy

into the speech and promote its central message:
the media team, plus the internal communications,
government relations, investor and industrial relations
teams. So speechwriters need to be able to work with
small or large groups of people to advance the unifying
narrative. If the speech is good enough, it can lead
the way for the whole enterprise, providing the long-
form language that all the other departments can draw
upon for their own communications. Even so, the
speechwriter herself is unlikely to fit seamlessly into
any institutional culture – not even when working in
a political office for a politician they greatly admire.
Speechwriters won't toe the line. They won't blend into
the hierarchy. They will always take an irritatingly high-
minded view. And they can be irritatingly precious and
oversensitive to criticism.

Never forget, however, that the speechwriter is your
enterprise's best friend. Because when all others falter, they
still cleave to the higher purpose. Speechwriters keep the faith.
They believe in the power and importance of leaders, and in
the possibility of changing the world for the better through
the power of words. If you are lucky – and leaders often are –
your speechwriter will one day write your biography and
cement your place in history. All she ask of you is the chance
to help you make it happen.

The collaborative process

When a speechwriter is engaged, the process begins with the client briefing. This briefing can take various forms. Often I will sit down with the client and they will talk me through what they want to say in detail. Sometimes the briefing will have a relaxed interview format, in which I initiate the questioning and we go back and forth on the topic until I am sure the client and I have an agreed sense of the terrain. After the discussion, I ask for any other relevant documents, including recent financial results, in-house presentations and maybe a news article or two. I go away, do the reading and thinking, draft the speech and email it through. The client amends it, adding personal anecdotes and relevant statistics. We might go back and forth a bit by phone or email, before the client delivers the final speech.

But there are times when it is not so simple, such as when a senior communications manager emails me a document consisting of bullet points, described as an 'outline' of the speech. The implication is that the hard intellectual work has been done and all I need to do is add extra words, like being handed a colouring-in book and told to fill in the lines with a few decorative splashes of colour. This is usually not very helpful, because I often discover that joining the dots just creates a list of ideas, not a cogent argument.

Or else the outline reflects what the organisation would *like* the listeners to hear (the organisation is doing very well, its plans are on track, its people are excellent and very happy at work every day). It's a form of corporate magical thinking:

if I say it loudly enough, it must be true. But persuasion doesn't work by mere declaration.

Smart leaders understand the intellectual heft of prose. The CEO of Amazon, Jeff Bezos, for example, has vetoed the use of PowerPoint decks in his senior meetings. Employees are required instead to lay out their case in a formal note, rather like a press release (or a speech). That makes sense to me: the real thinking is never found in the bullet points, diagrams or declarations – it's found in the sentence-by-sentence build-up of argument that weaves together the assertions and the underlying proofs.

Then there are the times when the drafting of a speech is being overtaken by events – say, if the company is in the midst of sensitive commercial negotiations. Or the person giving the speech is just too busy to focus on it properly until the last minute, by which time they have changed their mind about what they want to say. Or the topic gets changed suddenly. Or an entire speech must be delivered at very short notice, perhaps in a crisis. Or an overnight media report changes the environment into which the speech will be delivered. Or there's a broader share market slide.

In these high-pressure situations I'll often have a phone conversation with the speaker, who is usually so busy they will have eight other things they simultaneously need to be dealing with. We'll talk, and quickly. I'll listen so hard that my ear is aching by the time the call ends, and my hand throbs from the effort of recording their words as fully and accurately as possible.

Actually, when you read speechwriter memoirs you'd think it was always like this: a mad, blood-vessel-bursting rush to the finish every time. More often, however, speeches do develop in a relatively orderly fashion. In a well-organised outfit, the variables can be at least partly predicted. You usually know if a key number is going to come out that day, or if a certain business development is likely to be concluded or postponed. And where there are changes required, it's a matter of simply amending specific sections of the speech rather than wholesale rewriting.

The entire process improves as the client and the speechwriter get to know and trust one other. The first few speeches I do for someone normally require a lot of input from them. I need to know what they care about, how they like to talk, what they want to achieve. But once I know those things, it's relatively easy for me to devise good first drafts. That reduces the pain a lot.

'Go do your magic,' one client used to say, airily.

When I first went to work for Kim Beazley, for example, it was a comparatively straightforward process because I was working with his long-time staffers, and there was a solid body of Beazley speeches and media remarks that I could draw upon. After a few months, I got to know Beazley myself and came to understand his values and his broad views on most topics. He was good at reviewing drafts and would improve them considerably.

But there were times when he was so busy he would have no time to review a draft thoroughly. Instead, Beazley would skim the text beforehand and then (I suspect out of courtesy to his speechwriter) politely read the speech aloud in full, while improvising his own lengthy additions along the way. This sometimes tested the patience of even the most partisan audience. In those days, I was too young and nervous to pick him up on this habit. Now I would, and I'm sure he wouldn't mind either (although he might well have ignored my advice anyway). But that's the benefit of age.

Encounters with a new client

When I am starting out with a new client, I always prefer to meet (or speak) with them for the first time on my own. This gives the client an opportunity to drop their guard a little and talk frankly to a relative outsider. But that is a rare luxury. More often there's a corporate communicator close by. Still, a good communications adviser understands what I need to do to make the process work. As we begin the conversation, first of all, I am listening to the client's style of speaking:

- Is it fast or slow?
- Are the sentences long or short?
- Where do they breathe in a sentence – in the middle or at the end? I don't want to mimic them, but I will adapt to their way of communicating.
- Are they highbrow or lowbrow users of language?
  Do they use academic or business jargon? Are they
  imaginative or conventional in their choice of words?

I particularly want to know where they find their metaphors, so sometimes I'll ask the client to give me an analogy: 'That's very interesting. What would you compare that challenge to ...?' I wait for Everest, or the grand final, or a marathon, or, if I'm lucky, something more interesting. Once a speaker compared the task of running a diverse company to conducting an orchestra of talented people playing different instruments. That surprising and generous image said a great deal about that speaker's personal style and leadership approach.

I also listen for signature words or phrases that seem to express the personality of the speaker; later, I'm told that I've really captured someone's voice when all I've done is incorporate a few minor linguistic idiosyncrasies.

God forgive me, I have even used 'going forward' in a speech because I knew that would feel completely true to the speaker, and would make them relax.

I'm also listening for evidence of self-destructive tendencies, such as when the speaker says loudly that they want to publicly defend their recent exorbitant bonus payment. *Ah, no.* Or they want to publicly name and lambast that journalist who is writing a series of articles on the company's poor customer service standards. *Hmmm. I don't think so.*

Sometimes I am forced to urge caution when a client gets carried away by the idea of the great line; that killer sentence which, like a beautiful but poisonous plant, must be weeded out. Even if I came up with that line in conversation myself. Perhaps especially then. (On the other hand, there have been times when I have come up with the perfect and completely defensible line and my client has apologetically rejected it on the grounds that it will be too newsworthy: they'd rather not attract that much publicity. I say more about one-liners, and how they work, in Chapter 6.)

As a speechwriter I have my own equivalent of the Hippocratic Oath: first, do no harm. Get the facts right, don't offend anyone unless you fully intend to (and understand the consequences of so doing), and don't commit your speaker to something they can't deliver.

Sometimes I will sit down with an anxious new leader who doesn't yet know how to work with a speechwriter at all, and can't begin to tell me what they want to say. So we go back to basics. I ask them:

· What is your priority right now?
· How do you spend your time?
· What's your biggest threat or opportunity?
· Where do you see the business in five years?

Suddenly we're talking and we're thinking in bigger, broader frameworks. Some will offer to talk in general terms about the kinds of things they want to address in their speech – 'I'll give you a brain dump, shall I?' – leaving it to me to formulate a structure later. Other leaders manage the complexity of their roles by being highly structured in all aspects of their life and even in their everyday communications, so they decide to talk me through a detailed proposed structure for a speech, perhaps even handing me their notes. But, as so often happens, I'll see that it's not a speech structure they've given me at all – it's a record of their thinking process, culminating in the main message. The task of the speechwriter is to flip the order, and make sure the main message is up the front and structures the entire speech.

Often I see that corporate strategy arises from a series of decisions, not the other way around. So we move outwards from concrete actions to larger frameworks. Then I will have to go away and get all this down into 20 minutes of purposeful talk. Consider, craft, refine, and edit.

Discovering that elephant in the room

And there's one more thing to bear in mind, for the modern speechwriter confronts a rather curious problem. Far from being the lead spin-doctor, she can easily become the unwitting *victim* of spin. This is not necessarily deliberate misdirection (although it can be). Sometimes it's just that in the briefing process the speechwriter might not be given all the necessary information – the warts-and-all truth – by either the speaker or their team.

Corporate leaders desperately want to believe their own good-news story and will psychologically downplay anything that might undermine it. They think they are hard-headed when in fact they are easily seduced by their own rosy version of reality. And that is how the enterprise culture commences its slow detachment from the tangible world, and fails to notice that great big elephant in the room.

One way in which more sophisticated enterprises try to manage this risk of blindness to the obvious is to do what politicians do: they pay pollsters and market researchers to give them objective feedback from all the different stakeholders. You might think that would guarantee a swift reckoning with reality. Even then, however, with the hard evidence right there in front of them, the feedback can be so painful they choose not to believe it.

So one task for the speechwriter is to uncover the truth. It's like being a detective, or a psychologist, or a spy.

The client – the speaker or perhaps the communications chief – starts out by telling me the good-news story about the business, the story they think a speech should tell. Okay, fine. I let them go on. I ask a few questions. I wait. Then after a while, they relax. They forget about the speech. They fill in some background. They tell me some war stories. Gradually, sometimes inadvertently, they begin to give me a fuller picture. Eventually, slowly, out it all comes: the mishaps and compromises, the risks and challenges, the scale of dissent and the efforts to overcome it. And that's when, nine times out of ten, just as it is getting really interesting, they will stop and say, 'Oh, but you can't mention *that* in the speech.' That's when I know we have met an elephant.

For example, the telecommunications chief executive will tell me that they are ready and proud to announce the new direction of the company. What they are less inclined to reveal is that this bold new direction has been forced upon the business by the huge losses incurred by the CEO's failed Asia strategy.

Or it's the grand opening of the new wing. But it transpires that the company is actually years behind schedule and the lead contractor was sacked, and due to cost pressures the company is opening the building before it's quite finished.

Or the bank CEO is pleased to announce that the bank is opening many new branches. But the backstory is that the bank is merely re-opening some branches that were shut down during an era of ruthless cost-cutting. The bank has finally accepted that the cost savings were outweighed by the loss of customers.

All too often I see companies that don't want to acknowledge there is a problem at all, not even in the privacy of drafting a speech. It's partly, I suspect, because people who can't write well simply cannot imagine how a difficult or sensitive issue might be addressed in a public speech without causing some kind of disaster.

There's also a common misapprehension about the fundamental nature of a good speech. A speech is not a monologue; it is a dialogue. It reflects a careful process of listening in advance to the feelings and attitudes of the audience. I learned this the hard way. I once dated a man who justifiably accused me of 'speechifying' at him. My speeches were irrefutable elucidations of the problems in our relationship and my proposed solutions. These speeches were not genuine communications – they were long on incriminating facts against the boyfriend, but short on what was really going wrong between us, because I never engaged sincerely with his side of the story. I won the argument but lost the affection. Corporations often make the same mistake.

More pragmatically, there are always going to be those people in the know; the ones who are across the full details of the ugly backstory. They may be members of staff, or analysts, or customers, or journalists. And if there are such people, chances are that one of them, sometime, is going to go public with their grievance. So it's always a greater risk to ignore an unpleasant fact than admit to it. It is absolutely possible to write in such a way that, far from causing more problems, acknowledging a sore issue will create confidence, leading to a perception in the audience that the CEO is realistic, well informed and grounded. Deciding to articulate a problem may also result in devising a solution that makes the company even stronger and better placed to articulate and defend its strategy in public.

America's giant discount store Walmart had a long and proud history of low prices and good customer service. But as the world's biggest retailer, with enormous scale and purchasing power, Walmart had an abysmal record on the environment. Pressure was growing for change. After a year of planning and consultation, in 2005 CEO Lee Scott used a major 5000-word speech entitled 'Twenty First Century Leadership' to tackle the elephant in Walmart's room. He announced a suite of major environmental initiatives and targets, including being supplied by 100 per cent renewable energy, creating zero waste, and using Walmart's supply-chain power to sell products that sustained people and the environment.

The key to the success of that speech was that Lee Scott presented the environmental U-turn not as an abrupt shift for the company, but as a natural extension of its people's core values. Scott anchored his speech in the story of Jessica Lewis, the co-manager of a Walmart store that was located at the epicentre of the chaos that had recently been caused by Hurricane Katrina. Lewis was a hero:

That night, though it was dark and flooded, she took a
bulldozer and cleared a path into and through that store,
and began finding every dry item she could to give to
neighbors who needed shoes, socks, food, and water. She
did not call the Home Office and ask permission. She just
did the right thing. Just like thousands of our associates
who did the right thing, a trait I am proud to say is bred
in our culture.

By using this story, Scott showed that he was paying attention to his people and learning from their example. He did not link Hurricane Katrina directly to the effects of global warming. But the inference can be clearly drawn. Walmart had at last opened itself up to climate change realities, and to the burden of its modern-day corporate responsibility. Scott acknowledged that in the past Walmart had taken a 'defensive posture'. Now, by linking its new environmental approach to the best qualities of Walmart people, Scott was able to convert a painful recognition of past management negligence into a inspiring step forward for the whole company.

Here's another example. I once worked on an industry conference speech with Jens Goennemann, at that time the dynamic, pragmatic regional chief executive of a global defence manufacturer. Now, defence manufacturing is a particularly tricky business because in any national market there is only one client, one customer, one buyer: the national government. And if things go wrong with that government client, well, there's no other client to turn to. The business grinds to a halt. In the case of this company, one of several long-term projects for the government had not been going well. The product itself was excellent, but the manufacturer's supply lines weren't working. There had been long and unexpected delays in the delivery of spare parts, which meant that operational performance was well under the standard required. The government client was not happy. This was a worry for the long-term relationship. From the company point of view, however, the government too could have done better by being more flexible about working with them to solve the ongoing problems. So how could a speech address these complexities in a truthful yet productive way, and restore the relationship?

Goennemann, his chief of staff and I had long discussions and went through several detailed drafts to come up with exactly the right language. It was important to acknowledge the shortcomings of the company in a completely frank manner, but he had to do so without self-abasement, which might undermine confidence in his company's future capabilities. It was also important to be clear that the solution to the problems required effort from *both* parties, and to say this without unduly criticising or offending the customer. And most of all, it was important to steer confidently towards a resolution that would work for both sides.

Goennemann managed these complexities by talking from the outset about the enduring principles of *all* good long-term partnerships. He then went through the history of the numerous projects between his company and the government that had been successfully completed, or were ongoing and working well. He specifically identified a difficult point in each of these projects where things had gone wrong, and defined exactly how the matter had been fixed. It was only then that he referred explicitly to the problems in the current project, and how his team was working hard and, he believed, effectively, to resolve them, in partnership with the client. He suggested some further measures to improve processes into the future.

The speech was truthful and realistic. And it was well received by a hitherto sceptical government client.

Does knowing about the elephant in the room mean the speech must explicitly mention it? Maybe yes, maybe no. Often not. But I'd certainly be thinking about the risks of *not* mentioning it. And if I didn't mention it, I'd be thinking of other subtle ways to respond to any sensitive issues. Ignoring the other point of view is usually the worst option of all.

Case study

Vanquishing the elephant: Queen Elizabeth I in 1588

In 1588, England was under a very real threat of invasion and mass destruction by the Spanish Armada. The English Army had gathered at Tilbury to await the expected enemy landing. Queen Elizabeth arrived on her grey horse, dressed in white with a silver breastplate, to rouse her fearful troops to battle. She had been monarch for 30 years by then. Under her leadership, England had become relatively peaceful and prosperous. But now it faced an existential threat.

The Queen spoke while still seated on her horse. She began with a heartfelt statement of confidence in her troops' loyalty and gave a commitment to fight the Spanish alongside them, and if necessary, to die with them:

My loving people,
  We have been persuaded by some that are careful
of our safety, to take heed how we commit ourselves to
armed multitudes, for fear of treachery; but I assure you
I do not desire to live to distrust my faithful and loving
people. Let tyrants fear.

'Let tyrants fear.' What a line. She continued:

I have always so behaved myself that, under God, I have
placed my chiefest strength and safeguard in the loyal
hearts and good-will of my subjects; and therefore I am
come amongst you, as you see, at this time, not for my
recreation and disport, but being resolved, in the midst
and heat of the battle, to live and die amongst you all;
to lay down for my God, and for my kingdom, and my
people, my honour and my blood, even in the dust.

This is magnificent stuff. The monarch down in the muck and dust among her fighting men, ready to accompany them into battle, ready to give her all.

Then she said something extraordinary, something that pulls you up in surprise:

I know I have the body of a weak, feeble woman ...

What? Why on earth did she feel the need to say this? She had been Queen of England for 30 years; it wasn't as if the troops didn't know it was a woman under all that makeup. Why did she decide to deliver a very public reminder that she was a woman?

... but I have the heart and stomach of a king, and of a king of England too ...

Let us imagine the huzzahs that followed this line. And now she swelled, growing in ferocity:

... and think foul scorn that Parma or Spain, or any prince of Europe, should dare to invade the borders of my realm; to which rather than any dishonour shall grow by me, I myself will take up arms, I myself will be your general, judge, and rewarder of every one of your virtues in the field.

Time for some pragmatic motivation in the form of financial reward; she was, after all, a very practical woman:

I know already for your forwardness you have deserved rewards and crowns; and we do assure you on a word of a prince, they shall be duly paid.

Note that in this line she calls herself 'a prince'. Having acknowledged her weakness, she has now overcome it and assumed a virile young manhood. She concludes, as the leader must always conclude, with a message of confidence and hope:

In the mean time, my lieutenant general shall be in my stead, than whom never prince commanded a more noble or worthy subject; not doubting but by your obedience to my general, by your concord in the camp, and your valour in the field, we shall shortly have a famous victory over these enemies of my God, of my kingdom, and of my people.

Many modern advisers would have counselled Queen Elizabeth against making a point of the fact that she was a woman. She doesn't just draw attention to it, she overplays it, using not one but two adjectives, 'weak' and 'feeble'. She pushes the negative connotations of femininity extra-hard. She doesn't just shine a lantern on the problem, she also switches on the floodlights.

Here's my hypothesis. Queen Elizabeth must have taken the view that even her most loyal troops – those who adored their queen in prosperous peacetime – might be wondering whether a strong, young king would not have given England greater advantage in this moment of desperate peril. Well, she was not going to leave them to stew in their negative thoughts. She would not let them feel that their queen didn't understand the worst, most fearful and most ignoble imaginings that were going through their minds, and possibly undermining their fighting spirit.

So she raises *their* worst fears and *her* only weakness.

But in the naming of it, in defying her own weakness, Queen Elizabeth is doing more than demonstrating her sympathy with, and her understanding of, the misgivings of her troops. She is lending her 'weak woman's' courage to all those young and fearful soldiers. She is turning her own apparent weakness into their greatest strength.

Establishing the job of your speech

Often people like to seek my judgement on the latest speech – the one that everyone's talking about, the one attracting lots of media and social media attention. I am sure I sound rather feeble when I answer, as I usually do, 'I'm not quite sure what I think. Not yet, anyway.' Soaring oratory is not necessarily effective oratory – and effective oratory can be quite commonplace. It all depends on what you have decided is the job of the speech.

Advertising guru David Ogilvy liked to tell a story of the ancient Greek orators. When Aeschines spoke, Ogilvy would say, the crowds all murmured admiringly: 'How well he speaks.' But when Demosthenes spoke, they cried out: 'Let us march against Philip!' In his book *On Advertising* (1983), Ogilvy uses this tale to explain his philosophy of advertising:

> *When I write an advertisement, I don't want you to tell me that you find it 'creative'. I want you to find it so interesting that you buy the product.*

You might say that a speech can be judged a success if it meets the goal it sets for itself, if the desired audience chooses to 'buy the product'. To me, that seems about right, but not wholly right. There's a bit more to it, because the goal of most speeches can't be summed up quite as simply as 'buy this car or that toaster', or even 'choose war':

· Is it about the rapturous reception on the night?
· Is it about the media's coverage the next day?
· Is it about how often a speech is quoted over time, and whether the words or phrases enter the language?
· Is it about whether certain attitudes and values are shifted and changed?

Sometimes a speech can be very successful at the moment of its delivery, but not necessarily serve the interests of the speaker over the longer term. It seems to me that US President Barack Obama's presidency suffered, ironically, because of the very beauty of the speeches that got him elected. He was never quite able to be the president implied by the hope and promise of his rhetoric. He couldn't live up to the dream inspired by his own words. Of course, even if he had known this was going to happen, there was no way that young aspiring president would have downgraded his oratory, even if it meant paying for it later in terms of voter disenchantment. The oratory was too central to his electoral appeal.

More often than you might expect, it can be difficult for an outside observer to judge either the aims or the achievements of a particular speech. Even small ceremonial speeches can be based upon unexpected objectives. I once wrote a father-of-the-bride speech for a businessman. Usually the convention is that the father of the bride says some words in praise of his daughter, and in my briefing with the businessman, I duly got out my pen.

'Is she lovely?' I asked coaxingly, hoping for a few words of fatherly pride.

'She's a princess!' he shouted. 'You should see how much this thing is costing me! It's on a Greek island, God knows why. It's costing me a fortune, and apparently even the sun itself has been told to set on demand to provide the perfect backdrop for the photographs.'

Then he shook his head in disgust. 'No,' he said, 'I want this speech to make *my wife* happy. I just want to make *her* happy.'

I was surprised but not shocked. You hear many odd things when you are a speechwriter. 'Righto,' I said. 'Well, I have no doubt that making your daughter happy will be essential to making your wife happy, so let's see if we can do both ...'

If the aims of a wedding speech can be so difficult to assess, it's all the more challenging in a political environment. In 1994, when I was recruited as speechwriter to Kim Beazley's office, Chief of Staff Syd Hickman had a plan. In the almost certain event that Labor would lose the 1996 election and then Prime Minster Keating would retire, Hickman wanted Beazley lined up as the natural choice for leader of the opposition, with the objective of becoming Australia's next prime minister. To cement that idea in the minds of the caucus, the plan was to get Beazley elected as deputy prime minister when the incumbent,

Brian Howe, announced his retirement, which was likely to occur within the next 18 months, before the election.

Beazley had an excellent political mind, an unimpeachable political lineage and powerful union backers, and he was widely regarded as a very decent fellow. But he was seen by some in the inner circle as lacking the reformist drive and economic rigour that had characterised the greatest years of the Hawke and Keating governments. There was still a slight question mark over his leadership credentials.

Hickman's view was that a series of speeches would indicate Beazley's breadth and depth, consolidate his claim, and establish his values and priorities as Labor headed into opposition. Each speech would have its own specific job, but more important would be the effect that the *series* of speeches created – what they collectively demonstrated about Beazley's potentially prime ministerial breadth and maturity.

Over the following months, Beazley delivered the speeches as planned – on managing economic growth and the merits of privatisation; the new role of information technology in the delivery of public-sector services; the importance of Australia's multicultural agenda; the history and future of the Labor Party – and each speech turned up in the pigeonholes of Labor Caucus members rather like instalments of a top-flight reference for a job. And sure enough, Beazley was duly made deputy prime minister, and later Labor Party leader.

Case study

A quiet revolution: CRA Limited CEO Leon Davis in 1995

Here's a curious thing: a speech can be rather commonplace on delivery but revolutionary in longer-term effect. In 1995, Leon Davis, the CEO of mining giant CRA Limited (later Rio Tinto), gave a speech to the deeply conservative Australian Institute of Company Directors. The speech was titled 'New Competencies in Mining'. Now, is that not a dull title? You'd never pick that as the banner over ground-breaking oratory.

In the speech, Davis explained that the growth and success of the mining industry meant, paradoxically, that it was more essential than ever to have the support and understanding of stakeholders – employees, shareholders, Indigenous Australians whose traditional lands included the mine sites, and the general public. In 1993, the Australian *Native Title Act* had come into force, recognising the native title rights and interests of Indigenous Australians. Now it was time, said Davis, for mining companies to develop their so-called 'soft skills', including 'relationship-based competencies'.

Let me repeat that uninspiring phrase: 'relationship-based competencies'. Behind the bland human-resources jargon, Davis was actually arguing for a radically new and progressive partnership between the big miners and Indigenous communities that would respect the communities' rights, culture and heritage.

The key lines of the speech are these:

*From the referendum of 1967, when Aborigines ceased
to be statistical ciphers, to the* Mabo *judgement of 1992,
which effectively reversed the doctrine of 'terra nullius',
we have seen a major turnaround in public and official
attitudes ...*

*Instead of seeking ways a new development can
assist a neighbouring [Aboriginal] community once it
is operating, through our traditional 'good neighbour'
policy, we will be looking to collaborate in the design of
the project to maximise the benefits for both parties.*

*It's a shift in approach that acknowledges that
Aborigines are freshly empowered, and that they enjoy
community and government support. And it's a shift
that means that our geological, engineering and mine-
planning skills are going to have to be augmented by
skills in understanding and relating to community
concerns.*

Note the pragmatism. There is no emotional, political or moral
basis for the radical change of approach these unadorned words
represent. The need for change is offered simply as a response to
a change in circumstances, driven by the 'fresh empowerment'
of Aborigines and the shift in 'public and official attitudes'.

Davis understood his audience. He knew that appeals
to sentiment or justice would never work with hard-headed
corporate types. What would persuade them, however, was the
prospect of avoiding years of conflict and litigation instigated
by Aboriginal people that would distract from core business

and drive down mining industry profits. Davis used deliberately cool and unemotional language because he wanted to appeal effectively to his business peers.

The success of any speech that proposes such major change will rarely depend solely, or even mainly, upon the quality of the oratory. Great reformist speeches often succeed because of the broader communications and policy management before, during and after their delivery. That's why speechwriters need to work with other communications specialists and strategists, and ensure that the best possible conditions are created for the speech to succeed. Sometimes that will mean establishing several themes and principles in earlier speeches, or raising the key points in media interviews, or preparing staff through in-house communications – or all of these.

In the case of this particular reformist speech, Davis had laid the groundwork earlier in the year, in his first major speech as incoming CEO. 'Let me say this bluntly,' he had said to the business community in Melbourne. 'CRA is satisfied with the central tenet of the *Native Title Act*.'

He went on:

In CRA, we believe that there are major opportunities for growth in outback Australia which will only be realised with the full co-operation of all interested parties.
This government initiative has laid the basis for better exploration access and thus increased the probability that the next decade will see a series of CRA operations developed in active partnership with Aboriginal people.

Having laid that groundwork in March, Davis delivered the key speech in October, and followed up both these speeches with concrete, transformative action over the following years.

In her third 2012 Boyer Lecture, 'Old Barriers and New Models: The Private Sector, Government and the Economic Empowerment of Aboriginal Australians', Indigenous leader Professor Marcia Langton reflected on the mining industry's response to the High Court's *Mabo* decision and the subsequent native title legislation. She noted that Davis:

> ... *made a headland speech that shifted the industry's paradigm led as it was then by Hugh Morgan's Western Mining Corporation. Davis's acceptance of native title and tilt towards respect for traditional owners enraged Morgan and other industry leaders, but led to the sophistication in agreement making that we witness today.*

The Australian mining industry eventually came to be regarded as a world leader in forging mutually beneficial agreements with Indigenous communities. That apparently uninspiring speech by Leon Davis has come to be seen as the starting point for a genuine paradigm shift in relations between mining companies and Indigenous communities.

Case study

An unfulfilled opportunity?
Prime Minister Paul Keating in 1992

An interesting counter-example is another speech on Indigenous issues, this one the renowned Redfern Park Speech given by Prime Minister Paul Keating in December 1992. I live down the road from Redfern Park. It is a beautiful space, established in the 1890s, with large old trees and a stately fountain. Nowadays, one of Sydney's better bakeries lies over the road, but in 1992 it was still the heartland of Indigenous urban disadvantage.

Here are the famous words:

> *And, as I say, the starting point might be to recognise that the problem starts with us non-Aboriginal Australians. It begins, I think, with that act of recognition. Recognition that it was we who did the dispossessing. We took the traditional lands and smashed the traditional way of life. We brought the diseases. The alcohol. We committed the murders. We took the children from their mothers. We practised discrimination and exclusion. It was our ignorance and our prejudice. And our failure to imagine these things being done to us.*
>
> *With some noble exceptions, we failed to make the most basic human response and enter into their hearts and minds. We failed to ask – how would I feel if this were done to me? As a consequence, we failed to see that what we were doing degraded all of us.*

The speech provided a new way of talking about black–white relations. It complemented the landmark decision by the High Court of Australia in June 1992 to overturn the doctrine of terra nullius that had for so long justified the British land-grab of Australia. It reignited the hopes and dreams of all those who sought true reconciliation. And it has been acclaimed as one of the greatest speeches of Australian history.

The speech is also known because of a dispute over due credit. In his 2002 political memoir, *Recollections of a Bleeding Heart*, Don Watson, Paul Keating's speechwriter, recalled that he wrote the final draft of the speech and handed it to the Prime Minister, who reviewed the text over breakfast and delivered it in full on that fateful day. Keating took Watson's comments as an improper claim of ownership, and made his anger plain, not for the first time, when he wrote in a *Sydney Morning Herald* column in 2010: 'The sentiments of the speech, that is, the core of its authority and authorship, were mine.'

Tom Clark, a Labor speechwriter, author and academic, wrote an essay in *Overland* magazine in 2013 analysing the speech and the circumstances behind its creation. Granted access by Keating's office to that famous final draft, Clark noted Keating's few annotations to the text:

> *[Keating] scrawled changes to only a small number of words – for example, the manuscript's initial formulation on page 8, 'We took the children from their mothers,' has seen 'their' changed to 'the.'*

That shift from 'their' children to 'the' children is a small masterstroke: it brings the children closer; it converts them from belonging to a separate society that we might choose to ignore, to being part of our national community whom we have a duty to protect.

Keating and Watson are communicators with very different styles; Keating himself noted in his *Herald* piece that Watson was a prettier writer than he, though not a more pungent one. I think of the Redfern Park Speech as 'their' speech – a speech that could only have been produced by a visionary, risk-taking prime minister and his brilliant, historically literate speechwriter.

The curious thing is that for a speech with such major policy implications it had had startlingly little prior circulation or consultation. In *Recollections of a Bleeding Heart*, Watson noted that he held the speech close to his chest, saying he wanted to avoid being pressed to include a caveat to the effect that Australian history was no worse than the history of anywhere else. Watson did not want his words watered down. Every speechwriter understands this impulse. In his *Overland* essay, Tom Clark also referred to Watson's assertion that the draft had missed out on the regular level of 'office scrutiny', and that this enabled 'Keating the frontman to step outside the comfort zone of his office, leaving his staff to catch up with control of the message once it had gone public'.

I was working for Kim Beazley at the time the speech was delivered. My memory is that while it was immediately recognised as a great speech, in political terms it posed a problem that quickly became too big for any easy 'catch-up' once it had gone public. Labor insiders knew that, as Clark puts it, a 'large body of non-Indigenous Australians [regarded] Aboriginal reconciliation as a wanton distraction from the practicalities of government'. The speech reinforced a growing sense that Keating was preoccupied with issues of concern to the progressive left (such as the republican debate and the creative arts) while being out of touch with more prosaic matters that ordinary Australians cared about. That the speech had not even been passed in advance to the office of the Minister for Aboriginal and Torres Strait Islander Affairs just added to a growing perception that the Prime Minister and his office lacked political discipline.

The speech was certainly a gift to Labor's political opponents. It galvanised extreme right-wingers, and Australia found itself in the midst of an unedifying debate about whether we should be wholly proud or wholly ashamed of our past in the so-called History Wars. To be clear, the Redfern Park Speech was not itself arguing for unmitigated guilt:

> *Down the years, there has been no shortage of guilt, but it has not produced the responses we need. Guilt is not a very constructive emotion. I think what we need to do is open our hearts a bit. All of us. Perhaps when we recognise what we have in common we will see the things which must be done – the practical things.*

But ironically, the vivid language of the core section of the speech – with its use of that responsible 'we' – was so potent that it overwhelmed in the public mind the clarifying remarks. The perception that the speech expressed a 'black armband' view of Australian history was swiftly marketed and firmly entrenched by those on the other side of the argument.

By the time of the 1996 federal election, right-wing candidates with regressive social policies – people like Pauline Hanson – were emerging to unexpected electoral success. This in turn either forced, or gave an excuse for, newly elected Prime Minister John Howard to swing to the right on Indigenous issues. 'Now of course we treated Aborigines very, very badly in the past,' said John Howard to radio right-winger John Laws in 1996, 'but to tell children who themselves have been no part of it that we're all part of a racist bigoted history is something that Australians reject.'

If the Redfern Park Speech had been circulated to Cabinet colleagues or even around ministerial offices before its original delivery, it is certainly possible that attempts would have been made to water it down, as Watson feared, although I am inclined to believe that the Prime Minister would have held the line on the text.

But in the absence of any prior Cabinet consultation or communication management strategy, the speech was delivered seemingly out of nowhere, and into a policy vacuum. In the speech the Prime Minister speaks movingly about 'the practical things' that need to be done to repair black–white relations. The achievement of the native title legislation in 1993 was certainly a major progressive step. But Labor would have a substantial three more years in government before losing the election in 1996. The government's efforts towards practical reconciliation – measures that improved daily lives – would now be judged against the huge expectations set up by the speech, and inevitably found wanting by some.

The Redfern Park Speech remains a symbolic milestone, but perhaps we can reasonably ask whether it also represents an unfulfilled opportunity.

Choosing your vantage point

One of the most important decisions to be made in constructing any speech is the selection of the vantage point, and that decision becomes clear in the opening paragraphs. The vantage point will play a major role in determining the shape, context, meaning and impact of the rest. If I get it right, the speech will soar. If I get it wrong …

Imagine, if you will, that you are standing at a busy Sydney CBD intersection. Your phone rings and someone asks you to describe to them the lay of the land. You look around. You quickly note the signs on the nearby shops, the traffic lights, cars inching along in the mid-city jam, details of people on the move – a beard, a pram, a red shirt.

But soon you realise your vantage point is inadequate, so you go into a nearby building and head up a few levels. Here, you walk past middle managers at their desks and look out the window. Now you can see that one block back from the intersection, shoppers are queuing wearily at the taxi rank; a truck has stalled, which is causing that snarl at the right-hand turn; office workers are irritably picking their way around some hoardings.

But the picture still isn't very informative, so you go up higher until you find yourself walking past senior managers, and now you enjoy a wide-ranging view. You can see that, behind the hoardings, the development of the latest city building is well underway; you peer along the main street to the blue harbour and the white hull of a cruise ship; and you look back the other way and see the jumble of signs of Chinatown. You have much of the shape of the city in your head.

But if you are the leader and are asked to describe the lay of the land, even this elevated perspective is not enough. You've got to go to the very top of the building, because only at 360 degrees and 30 floors up can you see the true structure of the city as it nestles between harbour and mountains. And now you don't just have a vantage point in space, but also a vantage point in time. You observe that the weather is about to change as the darkening clouds move swiftly across the ocean; you note how many container ships are queuing to come into port; you spy the wisps of smoke over the distant bluish mountains, signalling the last days of a bushfire. Finally, you have all the context you need to describe the lay of the land as a leader should convey it. Not just what is happening now, but the changes that have occurred and will soon take place across the whole terrain.

Once you get to the top, it's your privilege and duty to have the leader's vantage point – to see everything from the widest panorama right down to street level. The leader is in possession of that core attribute of leadership: far-sightedness.

That's the leader's vantage point, and it encompasses past, present and future.

But the vantage point taken within any particular speech is more than just a matter of that broad perspective. A lot of people might think – and I've seen plenty of presentation gurus say – that you should always start from 'now' and project forward, that a speech is invariably about the push to the future. Even if you accept that premise, you have to define what you mean by 'now', and the best way to do that is often with reference to how you got there – the history, the backstory, the arc of the journey.

The choice of vantage point makes a huge difference to a grand political address. But it is also important to any speech delivered by a corporate CEO. Where do I start? *Last year's results? When I became CEO? When the company first opened its doors? The 2008 financial crisis?* Even the stump speech – the reiteration of the core company pitch – must be renewed on every occasion it is delivered, to rediscover its relevance via the right vantage point for that particular day.

If in doubt, there are some practical tools you can use. Think about space and time. Where is the speech taking place? What's that place like – the local weather, the geography? Is there anything in the design of the building? Surrounding streets, local landmarks? The values of this region, this city, this place?

If you write a speech for the National Press Club in Canberra, for example, you can take a nation-wide vantage point, appealing to the patriotism you will always find in that audience of press-gallery journalists and bureaucrats. Just say you are giving a speech about communications issues. To a Sydney or Melbourne audience you might set up your argument with the proposition that 'communications reform will bring better results to Aussie customers'. At the Press Club, however, you could go far higher and declare that 'communications reform will be critical to our nation's future'.

Then there's the occasion. If you are delivering the 'John Monash Oration', for example, you can take lessons from the life of Australia's genius soldier–engineer and talk about managing complexity, or leadership under pressure. Or it may be you are speaking at the Australian–American Chamber of Commerce, which might suggest an opening theme around alliances, or friendship, or partnering.

Even more potent and powerful is the use of time in a speech. It's possible to find an angle in time for any speech:

On this day a hundred years ago (or five, or one) ...

Or even a future angle:

Next week (or in five weeks' time) ...

As you are thinking about the draft, ask yourself: *What's going on in the world right now? What's in the news this week, this morning? Any anniversaries? Major events coming up? Shifts in the share market? National budget announcements? Elections? Sport?* Speeches don't occur in a vacuum, they occur in time and space. Make use of the moment to make your speech memorable.

Case study

The close-up vantage point:
Prime Minister Winston Churchill in 1940

For some speeches, the ideal vantage point seems straightforward, even unarguable. An incident occurs that must be addressed. On 19 May 1940, Winston Churchill gave his first radio broadcast as prime minister to the people of Britain. The situation was dire. The Netherlands had just fallen and the Germans were mowing down French, British and Belgian troops on the continent. The job of the speech was to let the British know exactly how badly things were going, and to start preparing them for the dreadful losses and sacrifices ahead, without overwhelming or demoralising them. Churchill had already delivered his famous 'I have nothing to offer but blood, toil, tears and sweat' commitment when he asked the House of Commons to support his new cross-party government a week earlier. Now, in this radio address, he got straight down to business.

He opened by briefly reminding his listeners what was at stake at this perilous time:

> *I speak to you for the first time as Prime Minister in a solemn hour for the life of our country, of our empire, of our allies, and, above all, of the cause of Freedom.*

He then headed immediately into the dark heart of the struggle:

A tremendous battle is raging in France and Flanders.
The Germans, by a remarkable combination of air
bombing and heavily armoured tanks, have broken
through the French defenses north of the Maginot Line,
and strong columns of their armoured vehicles are
ravaging the open country, which for the first day or two
was without defenders. They have penetrated deeply
and spread alarm and confusion in their track. Behind
them there are now appearing infantry in lorries, and
behind them, again, the large masses are moving forward.
The re-groupment of the French armies to make head
against, and also to strike at, this intruding wedge has
been proceeding for several days, largely assisted by the
magnificent efforts of the Royal Air Force.

Churchill used this extreme level of detail to bring home to the British the immediacy and urgency of the danger they faced. Having established the seriousness of their circumstances, he moved on to encourage the people of Britain to take heart in the fighting strength of the Allied forces:

We must not allow ourselves to be intimidated by the
presence of these armoured vehicles in unexpected
places behind our lines. If they are behind our Front,
the French are also at many points fighting actively
behind theirs. Both sides are therefore in an extremely

dangerous position. And if the French Army, and our own Army, are well handled, as I believe they will be; if the French retain that genius for recovery and counter-attack for which they have so long been famous; and if the British Army shows the dogged endurance and solid fighting power of which there have been so many examples in the past – then a sudden transformation of the scene might spring into being.

But as we know, there was to be no sudden beneficial 'transformation of the scene', and Churchill knew very well that it was almost inevitable that things would get very much worse. In fact, planning had already quietly begun for the retreat to Dunkirk. So he moved on:

It would be foolish, however, to disguise the gravity of the hour.

Again, this was carefully balanced by:

It would be still more foolish to lose heart and courage ...

Churchill's selected vantage point was the urgent *now*. This enabled him to establish himself as the voice of authority on the facts of the war as it unfolded. It also enabled him to impress upon the British that from now on, life was to be a day-by-day proposition. And his main message?

Having received His Majesty's commission, I have
formed an Administration of men and women of every
Party and of almost every point of view. We have differed
and quarreled in the past; but now one bond unites
us all – to wage war until victory is won, and never to
surrender ourselves to servitude and shame, whatever the
cost and the agony may be.

From highest to lowest, they would put their squabbles behind them and share 'one bond' in this 'solemn hour'. They would work together, hour by hour, waging total war until victory or death.

Through his use of this immediate and urgent vantage point, Churchill was helping the British not only to come to terms with their circumstances, but also to recognise that he would be their trusted source of information, as well as their commander, solace and where necessary – as they would discover – scold.

Case study

A revolution by vantage point:
President Abraham Lincoln in 1863

There are times when a leader chooses *not* to select the obvious vantage point of a speech. Take the Gettysburg Address. Lincoln's task was to participate in the dedication of a cemetery for the soldiers who had died in the appalling Battle of Gettysburg of 1863, which was a turning point in the American Civil War. You might think of various, entirely logical vantage points from which to commence such a speech. The battle itself, for example. At a stretch, maybe a step back to the commencement of the Civil War. Or, at the most abstract level, the US Constitution, because the argument about union versus state rights (and therefore slaveholding rights) had precipitated the war and would define its outcome. Or so it was thought.

As we know, Lincoln chose a very different vantage point for his speech:

> *Four score and seven years ago, our fathers brought forth on this continent a new nation, conceived in liberty, and dedicated to the proposition that all men are created equal.*

Lincoln's reference to the Declaration of Independence, with its radical defence of liberty and equality for all men, established entirely new parameters for understanding the issues at stake in the Civil War. After all, unlike the Constitution, the Declaration included no comfortable ambiguity about the acceptability of slavery: 'We hold these truths to be self-evident, that all men are created equal ...'

Moreover, in that one opening sentence of the Gettysburg Address, Lincoln changed the future of the United States by ensuring that henceforth the Declaration of Independence would be understood as its founding spiritual document, rather than the black-letter law of the Constitution. 'For most people now,' wrote Garry Wills in his excellent *Lincoln at Gettysburg* (1992), 'the Declaration means what Lincoln told us it means, as a way of correcting the Constitution itself without overthrowing it.'

From that vantage point, the entire meaning of the Battle of Gettysburg and the task of honouring the soldiers who died in that battle took on a different hue. It wasn't so much about winning the war; it was about something far greater. It was about ensuring that:

> *... this nation, under God, shall have a new birth of*
> *freedom – and that government of the people, by the*
> *people, for the people, shall not perish from the earth.*

Lincoln used that single decision – his choice of rhetorical vantage point – to change the way a nation saw itself.

Case study

The switcheroo: Prime Minister David Cameron in 2013

On 23 January 2013, British Prime Minister David Cameron gave a long-awaited speech setting out his approach towards the future of the European Union, and Britain's place within it. In crafting that speech, Cameron was faced with a very difficult situation. Within his own Conservative Party, the Eurosceptics were calling for Britain to withdraw from the European Union. The UK Independence Party (UKIP) was enjoying electoral success with its own even more extreme anti-Europe posture. And on the other hand, Cameron's minority government relied upon the support of its strongly pro-Europe Liberal Democrat coalition partner.

Cameron began his speech like this:

This morning I want to talk about the future of Europe. But first, let us remember the past.

So we have an immediate and arresting switcheroo of vantage point from the future to the past. It's now a double perspective, and that double perspective becomes more important as the speech goes on:

Seventy years ago, Europe was being torn apart by its second catastrophic conflict in a generation. A war which saw the streets of European cities strewn with rubble. The skies of London lit by flames night after night. And millions dead across the world in the battle for peace and liberty.

It's a dramatic portrait of Europe in ruins in 1943 – 'torn apart', 'strewn with rubble', 'lit by flames'. We wonder why Cameron chose to start with an image of breakdown. But he quickly moved on to emphasise the cooperative long-term work that was required – and achieved – to overcome that collapse and turn Europe towards peace and prosperity:

As we remember their sacrifice, so we should also remember how the shift in Europe from war to sustained peace came about. It did not happen like a change in the weather. It happened because of determined work over generations. A commitment to friendship and a resolve never to re-visit that dark past – a commitment epitomised by the Elysée Treaty signed 50 years ago this week.

With the reference to the 1963 Elysée Treaty, Cameron was reminding his audience that he had the broad leader's perspective, the one that encompassed all the diplomatic milestones of the post-war European project. And then he showed us that his ample historical perspective was enlarged by his own personal experience:

After the Berlin Wall came down I visited that city and I will never forget it. The abandoned checkpoints. The sense of excitement about the future. The knowledge that a great continent was coming together. Healing those wounds of history is the central story of the European Union.

Cameron here established his long interest in – and by inference, commitment to – the idea of a free, peaceful Europe. But the image of a young Cameron celebrating in 'abandoned' Berlin after 1989 comes daringly close to evoking a decadent Euro-cosmopolitanism. So Cameron balanced this, anchoring himself by association with Britain's most stubborn and beloved patriot:

What Churchill described as the twin marauders of
war and tyranny have been almost entirely eradicated
from our continent. Today, hundreds of millions dwell
in freedom, from the Baltic to the Adriatic, from the
Western Approaches to the Aegean.

Invoking Churchill was always going to appeal to Cameron's core conservative constituency. He even went further and used the old-fashioned World War I term 'Western Approaches', as if channelling one of John Buchan's very British, boys-own spy novels. He went on:

And while we must never take this for granted, the first
purpose of the European Union – to secure peace – has
been achieved and we should pay tribute to all those in the
EU, alongside NATO, who made that happen. But today,
the main, over-riding purpose of the European Union is
different: not to win peace, but to secure prosperity.

And now we get to the rather extraordinary main point:

The challenges come not from within this continent but
outside it. From the surging economies in the East and
South. Of course, a growing world economy benefits us
all, but we should be in no doubt that a new global race
of nations is underway. A race for the wealth and jobs of
the future. The map of global influence is changing before
our eyes. And these changes are already being felt by the

entrepreneur in the Netherlands, the worker in Germany, the family in Britain. So I want to speak to you today with urgency and frankness about the European Union and how it must change – both to deliver prosperity and to retain the support of its peoples.

Much has been written about this speech, and nearly all of it has focused on its positioning of the relationship between Britain and the European Union and, in particular, Cameron's promise that the Conservatives would hold a referendum on British continuation in the EU if they won the next election.

I find it almost as notable that Cameron painted a portrait of a Darwinian global future, and a struggle between Europe and Asia for wealth and jobs. It is a world in which even the wealthiest European nations would lose out to the emerging economies of Asia and elsewhere, unless the European Union faced up to the imperative of dramatic change.

And now perhaps we can understand why Cameron opened the speech with a stark image of Europe in collapse. Twice in the 20th century, Europe fell apart because of internal conflict. Now Europe was facing the prospect of a third catastrophic breakdown, this time because of challenges that came 'not from within this continent but outside it'. After all, the word-picture of a society 'torn apart', 'strewn with rubble', 'lit by flames' could be used to describe a failing urban centre suffering from a hollowing out of job prospects, social breakdown and the flight of capital and people caused by the relentless shift of resources and wealth to more competitive emerging economies.

Cameron went on to call for a series of European Union reforms, including extending the single market to 'services, energy and digital' and returning some powers to member states, particularly in the areas of workplace rules, the environment, social affairs and crime. His unspoken conclusion? If the European Union didn't respond to the competitive demands of our times and become more 'flexible, adaptable and open', it would face a third collapse as terrible as the first two. Cameron used his vantage point to paint a portrait of Europe's past and offer a dark premonition of its future if it did not tackle reform.

David Cameron chose Europe's history as the vantage point from which to argue the case for genuine change in the EU. But this eloquent speech failed to resonate with either the British public or European leaders. The British public voted for Brexit in March 2017. Time will tell whether that speech was just a failure, or also a prophecy.

Case study

Multiple vantage points: Walmart CEO Lee Scott in 2005

I referred earlier to the major address delivered by Walmart CEO Lee Scott in 2005 called 'Twenty First Century Leadership'. Under fire for their inadequate approach to corporate environmental responsibility, Walmart executives had been listening to critics and developing a considered and comprehensive response. When Scott announced the new plan, it was the first time the company had ever broadcast one of its speeches live to every staff member in every store, club and distribution centre.

Scott opened his address with a reference to the very origins of Walmart. There he was at the top of the building, overlooking both space and time:

> *Walmart started as one man's dream 43 years ago ... [Sam Walton's] method was to go where other businesses feared to go. The other retailers of that time were convinced they wouldn't make money in small town America ... We became Walmart by being different, radically different.*

But then came a second setup, this time a reference to the listening work undertaken over the prior year. Scott moved his vantage point down from the top to mid-level, demonstrating that he understood the local environment and was aware of how the company was viewed from the street:

> *Even with this great beginning, we have received our share of criticism over numerous issues, not the least of which is our size. After a year of listening, the time has come to speak, to better define who we are in the world and what leadership means for Walmart in the 21st century.*

And finally, Scott landed at ground level, where the speech finds its full power and strength. There he was in the thick of it, a leader at street level with his people:

When [Hurricane] Katrina hit last month ... I saw a
company utilize its people, resources and scale to make
a big positive difference ... Katrina asked this critical
question, and I want to ask it of you: What would it
take for Walmart to be that company, at our best, all
the time? What if we used our size and resources to
make this country and this earth an even better place
for all of us: customers, associates, our children and
generations unborn?

The speech went on to outline a dramatic suite of measures
and targets, primarily related to environmental action but also
addressing employee healthcare, community engagement and
workforce diversity.

And the plan unfolded as promised in the speech. As
the company moved closer to reaching its declared targets,
perceptions of Walmart slowly improved. The company
went from being seen as one dragging its feet on social and
environmental sustainability to one making a genuine effort.

The tripartite beginning to the speech represents a clever
and valuable sleight of hand. Walmart had clearly been planning
this set of announcements for at least six months. But without
in any way lying or misleading his employees, Scott led his
staff to connect their own experience of Hurricane Katrina –
the hardships and heroics that had taken place just a month
or so earlier – with a moral and material turnaround at the
highest level of the company. The speech changed the apparent
dynamic: instead of responding to its critics out of harsh

necessity, Walmart was stepping up to meet the highest ethical aspirations of its employees, as they had so ably demonstrated in a recent crisis.

You will always have to find your own specific entry point into every speech. I never, ever find the exercise easy, but I always find it immensely satisfying. Getting the vantage point right creates the organising principle for the entire speech.

Identifying your key audience

One of the injunctions that used to be given to novice speechwriters was to 'research your audience'. *Great. Fine. Um, which audience would that be?* In the modern world, everyone is the audience – or at least, no one isn't. Any speech can instantly be made available, in full or in part, to anyone with a mobile phone. Major speeches are live-tweeted – and even parsed – line-by-line. You cannot even trust that those speeches that are notionally in-house or under the code of silence of the Chatham House Rule will not be recorded and widely disseminated in some form.

This can all be completely paralysing to the writing process. You can waste your time drafting speeches that try not to offend anyone, line by tedious line. Or you can attempt to protect your speaker with jargon and hedged messages, which means they deliver boring, obscure and frustrating speeches.

If you make everyone your audience, then actually, no one is. So you have to harden up and make some choices. By defining the job of the speech, you will discover exactly who the primary audience will be. And once you have discovered that audience, you need to write to them:

- Your main focus is to push for changes to the regulatory environment affecting your industry? Well, the audience is probably going to be around 30 influential people in government working in that policy area.

- You want to get the share price up? The primary audience will be analysts and investors.

- You are deep in negotiations with the unions? You are speaking primarily to trade union leaders, and you need to couch your argument primarily in terms of the persuasions or threats that will be meaningful to them.

- You want to pin your lazy executives to some strategic goals? Announce those goals publicly and name the executives who will deliver them.

- You want to impress your doubtful board with your genius? That's a speech designed to allay the concerns of 10 people in time for the next board meeting.

Once you know what job the speech has to do, clarifying your main audience is quite a simple process.

One amusing pastime for this speechwriter is to watch a senior political figure give a speech and guess to whom the speech is actually directed. Sometimes you think, *Oh yes, it's to their own political base.* Other times it might be to win over those promiscuous swinging voters. Often it's a pep talk to their own cowardly, weak-kneed caucus, terrified by the latest polling figures. Sometimes you just wonder. But the more you play this game, the better you get at it and the more you understand each player's real political agenda.

Very often the real audience for a speech won't physically be in the room. They will be occupied elsewhere – in their high political offices, or regulatory agencies, or trade union headquarters, or out in the electoral heartland, far away from the overblown furnishings of the hotel ballroom where such speeches are typically made. I have written 25-minute speeches for leaders to deliver to audiences of 200 people, when the job of the speech was to influence just four or five absent bureaucrats or policy-makers.

It won't usually matter if there are no representatives from your target groups physically present on the occasion when a speech is delivered (although no doubt specific invitations could be issued to ensure they were in the room if you really wanted them to attend). The media coverage can do the job for you, and you can make sure the target audience members are made aware of the event, receive copies of the text, and get personally briefed on its contents.

It is also worth noting that a key audience may be those who will like your speech least. Successful leaders nearly always have opponents, if not outright enemies. As great politicians know, it's your enemies who define you. But the rhetorical challenge is to understand in advance exactly who you are going to offend, why, and whether it will be worth it. A speech can be judged a wholehearted success if it provokes the right opponents in the right way. This can crystallise the debate and galvanise support.

Case study

Playing against your audience: Alcoa CEO Paul O'Neill in 1987

In October 1987, the new CEO of aluminium company Alcoa, Paul O'Neill, gave his first big speech to investors and analysts in a New York hotel ballroom. This audience of commercial hardheads would have had very clear expectations of the kind of speech that O'Neill would deliver. They would have expected him to talk about his commitment to the creation of shareholder value, discipline on costs, and sources of market advantage. Instead – as recorded by Charles Duhigg, *New York Times* reporter and author of *The Power of Habit* (2012) – O'Neill took to the stage and said:

> *I want to talk to you about worker safety. Every year, numerous Alcoa workers are injured so badly that they miss a day of work. Our safety record is better than the general American workforce, especially considering that our employees work with metals that are 1,500 degrees and machines that can rip a man's arm off. But it's not good enough. I intend to make Alcoa the safest company in America. I intend to go for zero injuries.*

At this point, the audience was flummoxed. What on earth was this CEO talking about? One investor mentally labelled O'Neill a crazy hippie. O'Neill went on:

> *If you want to understand how Alcoa is doing, you need to look at our workplace safety figures. If we bring our injury rates down, it won't be because of cheerleading or the nonsense you sometimes hear from other CEOs. It will be because the individuals at this company have agreed to become part of something important; they've devoted themselves to creating a habit of excellence. Safety will be an indicator that we're making progress in changing our habits across the entire institution.*

Duhigg tells this story as an illustration of the power of creating a 'keystone' habit in an organisation. The disciplined emphasis on safety was to become a proxy or standard-bearer for better performance and discipline right across the company. But why did O'Neill choose to deliver this staff-oriented speech to the investment community instead of his employees? After all, his safety program was about employee wellbeing, and it would require the wholehearted input of employees if it were to succeed. It didn't seem to offer much to investors: when the CEO was talking about safety measures, he was talking about raising the cost of doing business.

This surprising tactic was, I think, inspired. Employees know that when their CEO speaks to the shareholder–analyst community, they are putting their personal reputation on the line in a way that never happens at any mere staff presentation. They are making promises for which they will be held to harsh account. Employees know just how often CEOs talk big to them about staff safety and wellbeing and do little about it. O'Neill was telling his people that he meant it. His employees were the real audience for the speech; Wall Street was the slightly horrified witness.

You could also say that O'Neill, even as he provoked his immediate audience of shareholders and investors to short-term dismay, was knowingly beginning a vital process of re-education. He was teaching this key group of stakeholders to think of Alcoa in a larger context. He was helping them to understand that a company able to demonstrate discipline at the most fundamental level of its operations would also be able to set and meet the targets required to achieve significant long-term shareholder value.

'Within a year of O'Neill's speech,' Duhigg wrote, 'Alcoa's profits would hit a record high. By the time O'Neill retired in 2000 to become Treasury secretary, the company's annual net income was five times larger than before he arrived, and ... all that growth occurred while Alcoa became one of the safest companies in the world.'

A speech can't be judged any kind of success at all if it doesn't persuade its key audience. But powerful persuasion for one audience may well involve challenging or alienating other audiences along the way.

Satisfying your secondary audiences

Having impressed your case upon your key audience, you will not want to offend or mislead the other stakeholders you want to keep onside but to whom you are not primarily speaking on that occasion. The way to manage this is to use your editing process to assess the likely impact of your words on those other stakeholders and devise a strategy to manage the consequences. Write your first draft strongly for your key audience, then run that draft by the experts inside your company – whether it is the investor relations team, the government relations team, or the commercial people dealing with the most valuable clients. Let them tell you of any interpretational issues that may need to be addressed.

There are a number of ways to deal with secondary audiences. One way is to 'step outside' the speech and address those stakeholders briefly but directly:

- 'There will be those who say this can't be done. I say to them in response ...'

- 'Today I have talked specifically about the benefits of our new initiatives to our customers, but I also want to acknowledge the benefits to [our partners/our people/our shareholders] ...'

- 'To the trade union movement, I say: we recognise your concerns and will be happy to sit down with you to discuss them ...'

Another way to deal with secondary audiences is via a pre-speech briefing or phone call to let these groups know what the speech will be about, and to allay any concerns about the consequences that may flow from it. The CEO might personally ring key clients or political stakeholders immediately before or after a speech to explain the context of the speech and outline what it means for them. Another way to clarify matters is via a follow-up opinion piece published by a relevant media outlet that deals specifically with areas of the speech that may cause concern to particular groups.

The employee audience deserves special attention. Often I'll see a major external speech circulated to staff without any accompanying commentary or context, when in fact it requires careful parsing and explanation. Sometimes this is a result of laziness, but often it's just because of the sheer exhaustion that accompanies the preparation of a major address, especially if it has share-market implications. It's important, therefore, to have a well-resourced and coordinated parallel plan to reinterpret the speech clearly to staff, recognising that they will read it with a different point of view to other audiences. Options to do this might include team briefings by senior people, or a carefully worded email or video from the CEO that is not just a rehash of the speech, but a clear explanation of its implications for the people of the organisation.

Making (or reshaping) your reputation

Speeches can't be analysed in the same way as the latest book club novel. When we talk about literature we tend to focus solely on the text, and our personal opinion about the author is mostly, or perhaps it would be more accurate to say, temporarily, put to one side. About some of the greatest authors, like Shakespeare and Jane Austen, for example, we know very little. But a speech is a different animal altogether. We can never take the speaker out of the speech. When Aristotle wrote his *Theory of Rhetoric* he explained that the character of the speaker – their *ethos* – represented one of the three core elements of rhetoric, alongside emotional impact – *pathos* – and reasoned argument – *logos*. So what is this vital attribute called '*ethos*'? In rhetorical terms, it consists of two aspects. The first is the pre-existing reputation of the speaker, the profile that precedes the speaker to the podium. The second is the reputation that the speaker earns through the way they present themselves in the speech.

Generally, speakers are presented to the audience with the professional title that best conveys their credentials for making this particular speech. They might be chief of this function, or vice-president of that division, or well-known advocate in this field. But the title is not as important as you might think.

For the speaker is also blessed – or burdened – by their own personal history as they walk to the lectern. The members of the audience may already have some half or fully formed opinions about this individual. The way they understand the speech will be substantially shaped by their perceptions of the speaker.

So the audience might be familiar with the well-known facts about the speaker's war record. The gossip about their finances. The drink-driving charge in their youth. Their track record of fiscal conservatism. Their habits of taking selfies and sending tweets. Their history of philanthropy. Their expertise in their field of medicine or music or policy-making. Their controversial second marriage. Their love of cricket or cycling. Their comparative anonymity. Their low profile or their love of media attention. Their cowardly silence in the big debates. The strange gaps in their biography.

A speechwriter will be fully alert and attuned to this reputation. And she will also be alert to how this reputation will mesh with the circumstances and delivery of the speech. A reputation as a social conservative will be an asset at some religious venues but not at an inner-city rally. A record of sporting achievement might be highly valued by a group of businessmen but not relevant to a roomful of visual artists. So *ethos* is not absolute; it is, to some extent, circumstantial. Understanding this will make a considerable difference to the way a speech is shaped.

Some people have attained such an exalted reputation that their presence is as eloquent as speech. In his retirement, Nelson Mandela's history and character was like an altar that he stood upon every time he spoke. In 2016 I watched as American feminist and activist Gloria Steinem, fine-boned and still utterly charismatic in her 80s, rose quietly to speak to a group of Australian women; she had to wait five minutes for the applause to die down before she could speak. The language of great moral leaders is simple, confident, pared back, high-level. They are operating at the highest, and most abstract, level of leadership.

But what do you do if you *don't* have a wonderful reputation to precede you? Or if people don't know enough about you to form an opinion of your character at all? Or if people don't think much of you? Well, there is another way to earn *ethos*, and that is through the giving of great speeches.

Case study

Speeches that make a leader's reputation: Prime Minister Winston Churchill in World War II and US Senate Candidate Barack Obama in 2004

When Winston Churchill was made prime minister in 1941, it was a reluctant British nation that took him on. He had a track record in office of major errors of judgement. Certainly Australians will never forget the disaster of the World War I Gallipoli campaign, of which Churchill was a primary architect. Nevertheless, Churchill was brought back from the political wilderness because he recognised – ahead of and more deeply than any other political leader – the risks to Europe and Britain posed by the resurgent Germany.

Churchill's job during World War II was easy to describe and enormously difficult to achieve. He had to silence the would-be appeasers at home and keep up national morale, while working furiously behind the scenes to bring America into the war on the British side. Churchill gained stature from his extraordinary wartime speeches. He held the nation together psychologically. He became the trusted source of information, the national scourge and spine-stiffener. But immediately after World War II, Churchill was famously, and by a large margin, voted out of office. The British felt Churchill had the *ethos* to be a wartime leader, but not the *ethos* of a peacetime reformer for a post-war nation.

Another example of a reputation formed through speechmaking is that of Barack Obama. In 2004, as a political candidate to represent Illinois in the US Senate, Obama delivered the keynote address at the Democratic National Convention in Boston. It was there that he declared, 'There's not a black America and white America and Latino America and Asian America: there's the United States of America.' His electrifying speech made his reputation. Then he talked his way into the White House through a series of entirely inspirational speeches.

Case study

Speeches that improve a leader's reputation: Prime Minister John Howard in 1996, opposition leader Simon Crean in 2003 and Lieutenant Colonel David Morrison in 2013

On a number of occasions I have seen an act of oratory dramatically improve the reputation or character of the speaker in Australian public life. In late April 1996, John Howard had been prime minister of Australia for just six weeks and was still very much in learning mode when a horrific massacre took place in Tasmania. A deeply disturbed lone gunman had taken a semi-automatic rifle, easily obtained under the laws of the day, and randomly killed 35 people and wounded 23 more at the Tasmanian tourist site of Port Arthur. As leader of a coalition government that included the pro-gun, rural-based National Party, John Howard made the difficult decision to argue for and prosecute a big change to Australia's gun laws. The new *National Firearms Program Implementation Act 1996* would restrict the ownership of semi-automatic rifles, semi-automatic shotguns and pump-action shotguns, and would introduce uniform firearm licensing.

With the wholehearted support of the Australian people behind him, the Prime Minister could have simply promoted his policy change in the media or public forums that were entirely supportive. But he also made the brave decision to make his case in person to an angry audience of 3000 gun-toting Victorians in the town of Sale. To loud jeers and hisses, the Prime Minister told the assembly that he was about to take away their weapons.

It took physical and moral courage for John Howard to face this crowd (even while wearing a protective vest on the advice of police, a decision which was unfairly criticised at the time, and an act of prudence which he later regretted). After all, these were the people who would be directly and negatively affected by his decision. They were visibly inflamed with anger, and regarded by Howard's own bodyguards as potentially highly dangerous. John Howard was not an impressive-looking individual; cartoonists regularly portrayed him as a midget with oversized eyebrows. I can't find any record of his speech that day, which I assume is because it was also unremarkable as a piece of oratory. But it was the turning up that mattered. On that day, the Prime Minister grew in moral stature. He went on to become one of Australia's longest serving prime ministers, holding office for another 10 years.

Here's another example, perhaps even more admirable. In the early 2000s, Australia's Labor leader of the opposition Simon Crean took the view that Australia should not be sending troops to Iraq, in support of US objectives, without the backing of a United Nations resolution. Crean had made his position known in the parliament, but this had had no effect on the decision made by Prime Minister John Howard to engage Australian troops in the Iraq invasion. In January 2003, Simon Crean spoke at Sydney Harbour as part of the formal farewell to the 350 troops aboard HMAS *Kanimbla*, about to set off for the Persian Gulf.

Crean told the troops to their faces that he did not support their deployment without United Nations backing. What a difficult thing to do. He then said:

> *But having said that I don't support the deployment*
> *of our troops in these circumstances, I do support*
> *our troops and always will, and that distinction is*
> *fundamentally important. The men and women*
> *of our fighting forces in a democracy are expected*
> *unquestioningly to accept the orders of the government of*
> *the day. You don't have a choice and my argument is with*
> *the Government, not with you. I know that you will give,*

through service and through your training, to the best of
your ability. You are a magnificent fighting and defence
force, you have been trained for it.

Labor speechwriter Dennis Glover tells the story of the drafting
of this speech in his *The Art of Great Speeches* (2011) and
goes on to note what a painful and emotional occasion it was
for Simon Crean as well as the soldiers and sailors he was
addressing. I watched that moment on the TV news that night,
and I would count that speech as Simon Crean's finest moment
in public life. His sincerity and candour were unmistakeable.

Here's a third example of *ethos*-building speechmaking. In
response to shocking evidence of misogyny and worse among
his troops, Lieutenant Colonel David Morrison, Chief of the
Australian Army, delivered a filmed address to all Defence
staff in June 2013 that was distributed publicly on YouTube
and created an immediate sensation. His face tight with rage,
his voice raspy and disgusted, Morrison looked straight at the
camera and spoke of:

> *... evidence collected to date [that] has identified a group*
> *of men within our ranks who have allegedly produced*
> *highly inappropriate material demeaning women, and*
> *distributed it across the internet and Defence's email*
> *networks.*

He went on to say (and I am quoting in full so that you can
apprehend the full force of his stark, powerful words):

If this is true, then the actions of these members are in direct contravention to every value the Australian Army stands for. By now I assume you know my attitude to this type of conduct. I have stated categorically, many times, that the Army has to be an inclusive organisation in which every soldier, man and woman, is able to reach their full potential and is encouraged to do so.

Those who think that it is okay to behave in a way that demeans or exploits their colleagues have no place in this Army.

Our Service has been engaged in continuous operations since 1999, and in its longest war ever in Afghanistan. On all operations, female soldiers and officers have proven themselves worthy of the best traditions of the Australian Army. They are vital to us maintaining our capability, now and into the future.

If that does not suit you then get out.

'Then get out.' An electric moment.

You may find another employer where your attitude and behaviour is acceptable, but I doubt it. The same goes for those who think that toughness is built on humiliating others. Every one of us is responsible for the culture and reputation of our Army and the environment in which we work.

If you become aware of any individual degrading another, then show moral courage and take a stand

*against it. No one has ever explained to me how the
exploitation or degradation of others enhances capability
or honours the traditions of the Australian Army.*

*I will be ruthless in ridding the Army of people who
cannot live up to its values and I need every one of you to
support me in achieving this.*

*The standard you walk past is the standard that you
accept. That goes for all of us, but especially those who
by their rank have a leadership role. If we are a great
national institution, if we care about the legacy left to
us by those who have served before us, if we care about
the legacy we leave to those who, in their turn, will
protect and secure Australia, then it is up to us to make a
difference.*

*If you are not up to it, find something else to do with
your life – there is no place for you among this band of
brothers and sisters.*

That is some speech. A speech of unrelenting clarity. The speech
of a soldier declaring war on misogyny. Morrison shared the
public acclaim that ensued with his gifted speechwriter, Cate
McGregor.

It is interesting to consider the political challenge inherent
in each of these three speeches: Prime Minister Howard,
personally telling gun-lovers that he was taking away their
guns; Simon Crean, attending the farewell of troops to a war
he did not support; the chief of army taking his own people
publicly to task. In each case, it was a risk. There would have

been far easier approaches. Howard could have avoided that audience altogether. Crean might have come up with weasel words. Morrison could have couched his language more tepidly. But each of these occasions enhanced and strengthened public perception of the character of the speaker, and also, critically, enabled them to pursue their agenda more effectively.

When silence is not the safer option

So we have been reminded of occasions where leaders took significant risks in giving speeches and their bets paid off in greater public stature. But it's fair to say that the lesson a more cautious reader might take from these case studies is that speechmaking is a risky business, and public silence is probably a safer option more often than not.

Certainly, when it comes to business, many leaders operate this way. Oh, they don't like to admit that it's about risk aversion. They prefer to style themselves in a more flattering light as the behind-the-scenes type of CEO – the modest, low-profile, hard worker. My view is that in the modern era this is simply not realistic. CEOs and chairmen may not be in public life by election, but they are nevertheless very much a part of the apparatus of modern democracies. Just as citizens now expect corporates to demonstrate social responsibility, they want leaders to demonstrate personal responsibility too. And a key way to demonstrate this personal responsibility is through public speeches.

And beyond this moral requirement lies a coldly pragmatic consideration. A CEO who cultivates personal anonymity can become a material risk for their organisation, because a low-profile leader will always find it harder to manage in the inevitable crisis. When that emergency strikes, they will have no choice but to be the public face of the corporate brand during the product recall, the industrial accident or the tragic event. And if they are nervous and inexperienced in public (as they will be), and if people don't know them (as they will not if these leaders haven't allowed themselves to be known through public appearances and particularly through speeches), such leaders will already have a trust deficit and find it harder to win and sustain the confidence that will help them manage through the crisis. Time and again I've seen companies flounder in an emergency, because the leader doesn't really know how to lead.

Business people might still be under the misguided illusion that their personal character and private lives are not terribly important factors in the performance of their leadership roles. After all, unlike politicians, they are not dependent on the whims of the electorate. As long as they keep increasing profit margins and the share price goes up, surely it doesn't matter what people think of them personally? But even when all they aspire to do is appease their shareholders, modern CEOs must still have the personal authority to bring a great many people along with them as they pursue their goals. And the curious fact is that some of the most influential of those people will have no direct financial investment in the business – like community groups whose suburb will be affected by a new development or welfare agencies concerned about rising costs for poor people. To win over these stakeholders, the leader will need to bring to bear their personal qualities as well as their business acumen. They need to persuade these stakeholders to follow them – or at least not oppose them – in order to achieve the commercial goals that will reward their direct shareholders.

I recall the case of one now-retired Australian business leader who had been a very successful CEO of a big company, and chair or director of many blue-chip companies. This leader used to boast to his peers that he never made a public speech. I first became aware of this when a senior businesswoman told me she regretted his decision, because he was particularly effective and would have had many useful lessons and insights to impart. I sympathised with her regret, because this leader was, in my judgement, not merely withholding the gift of his professional wisdom, he was also avoiding a duty that accompanies civic seniority. Meanwhile, business journalists reported with admiration this leader's reluctance to speak in public, representing it as a sign of a modest self-possession that refused the drug of public attention. As if the giving of speeches represented nothing more than vanity and self-promotion, when it is a core part of a leader's role.

And here's the thing. Ultimately, this failure to communicate had practical consequences for at least one of his many roles. A not-for-profit organisation of which he was chair came under severe criticism for a period. It was a small but painful crisis. Years later, a deputy of that organisation commented that life would have been far easier during that difficult time if this leader had been prepared to explain publicly what the organisation had been doing; to be transparent about the inevitable challenges and setbacks they faced and how they had been dealing with them, and to reassure a nervous public. He did none of that, and everyone in the organisation paid a price, at least temporarily.

You might imagine that it's a safer option not to give speeches. But if you do not take public responsibility for your decisions, and if you are not prepared to explain them personally in a thorough and considered way, then you relinquish an important part of your authority. And you may be creating a serious risk.

Winning over a cynical public

For those prepared to step up onto the public stage, I must acknowledge that the art of speechmaking is as challenging – perhaps more challenging – than it has ever been. As I mentioned in Chapter 1, no leader or would-be leader can set about writing and giving a speech these days without accepting that they will face a wall of cynicism. A chasm appears to have opened between those who are in positions of authority and the rest of us. The task is to understand the cause of this new and widening gulf, and figure out how to bridge it.

Here's an exercise we do in my university teaching classes. I put this claim up on the large classroom screen and we all take a good look at it:

Australia must maintain large-scale immigration programs over the next 20 years to ensure economic growth.

As a group we discuss how we would persuade a general audience to accept this argument, and quickly see that, taking the conventional view, it shouldn't be all that hard. If we look at the GDP numbers, we will find that economic growth clearly correlates with the rise of immigration. It's a simple matter of maths.

Now I ask my class whether this argument would be likely to win today. Some nod; others aren't so convinced. As for me, I am quite sure that this argument as it stands may have been perfectly alright some years ago but is now open to serious debate.

Which takes us to the next question I ask my students: 'What do you think is the assumption (or, as philosopher Stephen Toulmin called it, the 'warrant') that underlies this argument for high immigration?' Most will start by saying the assumption is, surely, that immigration is a good thing. But that can't be right. How can that be the assumption when it is the very argument that we propose to make? We stare at that sentence for a while longer until someone says, hesitantly, 'Could the assumption be that *economic growth* is a good thing?'

Yes, it could. Sometime in the 19th century, capitalism replaced the Gospels as our source of guiding belief, and it has since become the dominant organising idea for modern society. So much so that most of the people I write for aren't even conscious that the virtue of endless growth *is* an assumption. This cohort have enjoyed successful careers, based, with only a few blips, on the longest sustained period of economic growth in world history, so they are naturally converts. Most of their friends and contacts and colleagues and underlings will be in the same position.

Economic growth has become such an article of faith among people in leadership roles that the majority of them completely failed to spot the massive incoming wave of global discontent and disenchantment with capitalism, known in its modern form as neo-liberalism. This explains the shockwaves among the elite as electorates in democracies around the world began to reject the establishment and embraced politicians and parties with what seemed like crazy, foolish agendas, privileging non-economic factors like border integrity, sovereignty, the environment and social equality over purely rational economic goals.

Here's the point: the claim (that high immigration levels over the next years will secure economic growth) will fail if people no longer believe – or even if they quietly question – the underlying assumption that economic growth is an undiluted good thing.

Now you might say that a speaker can simply rely upon the expert data and thoughtful analysis of esteemed, independent organisations like the World Bank, the UN, the OECD or the Australian Bureau of Statistics to bolster their case. But these enterprises are now seen, rightly or wrongly, as suspect. The public doesn't trust them, either.

So how does a leader manage this conundrum? Not by trying to paper over the widening cracks in the public conversation between the top tier of society and the rest. Rather, by working their way through the issues in a patient, thoughtful, sustained way, and then by constructing an argument based on believable evidence.

So let's go back to the immigration scenario I mentioned. Here are some of the additional questions that might need to be asked, and carefully answered, in order to round out the case. Could we:

- Defend the GDP growth metric by pointing to the wider social benefits of GDP growth (more money for everyone's health, education, aged care), or alternatively by warning of the dire consequences of economic stagnation or recession, perhaps drawing on examples from other countries or from history?

- Remind people why the sources we've used for this evidence, whether the World Bank or the OECD, can still be trusted? If appropriate, openly note any shortcomings or likely biases in the data, while still defending the underlying value of the findings?

- Acknowledge opposing views, and address them specifically and without rancour? Admit that many people are understandably sceptical about endless growth and worried about related issues such as resource limits, global warming, and environmental destruction? Argue that economic growth need not be inconsistent with environmental protection; or perhaps more positively that GDP growth will provide a better opportunity for us to find solutions to environmental challenges; or take a different approach altogether and argue that there are very good reasons why economic needs should still prevail over environmental considerations? Or some combination of these?

This is all hard work, because modern persuasion is a complicated business. Any thorough argument must increasingly go back to basics and question the underlying assumptions. Those leaders who patiently take the time to interrogate, justify and explain the foundations of their beliefs, the quality of their sources and the evidence for their arguments will demonstrate that they are both trustworthy and self-aware. They will show that they are neither out-and-out elitists, nor mouthpieces of a thought system they have bought into but don't fully understand. In making a truly credible argument they will have harnessed the full power of proof, not only increasing their capacity to win an argument, but enhancing their own credibility along the way.

The power of refutation

One of the old sayings in both politics and business is that you should never give free airplay to the competition. I've worked with business leaders who won't even mention the name of a major competitor in public on the basis that it gives the bastards free publicity. When I worked in Canberra, Australian politicians from the major parties used never to mention the names of minor parties in speeches, because that was to risk lending those ratbags an unwarranted aura of legitimacy. (That all ended once they were forced into alliances with them, of course.)

An unwillingness to mention the opposition, however, is too often accompanied by an unwillingness to address their opposing policies and competing programs. You could call this taking the high ground, or you could say this just provides a convenient excuse not to bother arguing your case in full. Because one of the most effective ways to bolster your own argument is to show that you have listened respectfully to opposing views and can point out where and how they are wrong.

Case study

Dismantling the other view, not the other person: Shadow Secretary of State for Foreign and Commonwealth Affairs, Hilary Benn, in 2015

In December 2015 the British Parliament debated whether to grant the government authority to extend airstrikes in Iraq against the forces of Islamic State (also called ISIS or Daesh). It was a contentious issue. Despite the rise in IS-backed terror attacks in Europe, the British public were understandably very reluctant to get further into the mire of the Middle East, still bruised by the shameful memory of being drawn into the 2003 Iraq war on dubious grounds. The Conservative government largely (but not unanimously) supported the proposed extension of airstrikes; the Labour Party was divided on the issue, and Labour leader Jeremy Corbyn was resolutely opposed.

After 10 hours of debate, Hilary Benn, the Shadow Foreign Minister, rose to speak. In 14 minutes of terse, passionate and detailed argument, he comprehensively put forward the case for supporting the airstrikes, even as his own leader sat glowering in disagreement behind him. The Benn speech is an altogether remarkable piece of rhetoric. It is particularly notable for the forensic care with which Benn acknowledged then respectfully rebutted or neutralised opposing views, point by careful point.

Benn's refutations were particularly effective because they were so carefully nuanced. Wherever possible he acknowledged shared ground with those on the opposing side of the argument, and this was very important because nearly all of them were his own party colleagues. 'I share the concerns', Benn says, '... about potential civilian casualties. However, unlike Daesh, none of us today acts with the intent to harm civilians. Rather, we act to protect civilians against Daesh, which targets innocent people.' And then: 'Of course we should take action – there is no contradiction between the two – to cut off Daesh's support in the form of money, fighters and women, of course we should give humanitarian aid, of course we should offer shelter to more refugees ...' Further: 'I accept that there are legitimate arguments, and we have heard them in the debate, for not taking this form of action now ... But I say the threat is now and there are rarely, if ever, perfect circumstances in which to deploy military forces.'

Equally, Benn was not afraid to be unequivocal when it was warranted. 'It has been argued', he said, '... that airstrikes achieve nothing. Not so: the House should look at how Daesh's forward march has been halted in Iraq.' He also tackled the debate about whether mounting airstrikes in Syria against Daesh would be a wise move within the context of a complex civil war: 'To suggest that airstrikes should not take place until the Syrian civil war has come to an end is to miss the urgency of the terrorist threat that Daesh poses to us and others, and to misunderstand the nature and objectives of the extension to airstrikes that is proposed.'

Benn's use of refutations is a model because he does not seek to diminish or belittle those he disagrees with. He is always respectful. By focusing purely on the merits of the arguments, by being exact about the points of agreement as well as difference, he reinforces the strength of his own case.

Justify and motivate

Under pressure, we all have a natural tendency to become defensive. We try to hold our ground and justify our position. But the best communicators recognise that while a *justifying* argument can win grudging compliance, a *motivating* argument can inspire genuine endorsement.

Case study

Reigniting core beliefs: Shadow Secretary of State for Foreign and Commonwealth Affairs, Hilary Benn, in 2015

Hilary Benn used both justification and motivation in his Syria airstrikes speech and together they worked seamlessly to advance his case. But the motivation was only successful because the justification was irrefutable.

To *justify* his assertion that the government should receive authority to extend airstrikes against Daesh, Benn meticulously outlined all the procedural requirements that had been met. The conditions set out by the Labour Party had been adhered to. It was lawful under the relevant UN Security Council resolution, and he set out the number, paragraph and text of the resolution itself. Britain was under threat of more terror attacks, and Benn cited the Bataclan theatre massacre in Paris a month earlier as an example of what could easily happen (and indeed did happen, in May 2017, when the Manchester arena bombing occurred). Britain had obligations as part of a coalition of more than 60 countries trying to defeat Daesh. Moreover, this was not a new initiative but an extension of existing military action to an adjacent area.

So it was legitimate party policy; it was legal; it addressed a justifiable need; it conformed with existing British obligations; and it wasn't a major upgrade of British involvement. The justification was compelling.

Which meant that now Benn's speech could soar. Towards the end of his address he began to *motivate*, using galvanising arguments addressed first to his Labour colleagues:

As a party we have always been defined by our internationalism. We believe we have a responsibility one to another. We never have and we never should walk by on the other side of the road.

Having invoked core Labour beliefs, Benn broadened his outreach to the values of all British parliamentarians:

We are faced by fascists – not just their calculated brutality, but their belief that they are superior to every single one of us in this Chamber tonight and all the people we represent. They hold us in contempt. They hold our values in contempt. They hold our belief in tolerance and decency in contempt. They hold our democracy – the means by which we will make our decision tonight – in contempt. What we know about fascists is that they need to be defeated. It is why, as we have heard tonight, socialists, trade unionists and others joined the International Brigade in the 1930s to fight against Franco.

It is why this entire House stood up against Hitler and Mussolini. It is why our party has always stood up against the denial of human rights and for justice. My view is that we must now confront this evil. It is now time for us to do our bit in Syria. That is why I ask my colleagues to vote for the motion tonight.

Here Benn finished his speech and the House of Commons broke into spontaneous, sustained applause. I would never advocate that a speaker rely solely upon motivation, because that lends itself to an argument based upon emotion over reason. But Benn had earned the right to deliver those rousing and emotive final words – and even that potentially melodramatic accusation of 'fascism' – through the methodical way in which he had gone about making his case. The final motivating lines were the culmination of a careful, justifying argument.

5

Persuasive tactics and how to use them

IN THIS CHAPTER we inquire more deeply into the use of persuasive tactics. We look at the power of storytelling and how to harness it; the optimal balance of reason and feeling; and the uses of ceremonial speech to enhance a leader's reputation. We consider how to seize the oratorical moment, whether that may be an epoch-making opportunity or just capitalising on your place on the run sheet. We conclude with two emerging challenges for modern persuasion: the formal apology and the special case of the scientist.

Storytelling: the real story

Let's start with the power of story. Stories have certainly moved up in the world. These days you'll find them in all kinds of unlikely places – in boardrooms, among political research teams, in brand strategy meetings and leadership communications seminars. The talk is all about 'corporate messaging' or 'brand narrative' or 'the corporate origin story' or even how to create 'the killer story'.

This interest in the warm art of storytelling has a cold-blooded cause: quite simply, consumers have far too much choice. Whether it's a T-shirt or an airline ticket or a slab of butter or a car, most of the available products in each category these days are perfectly functional and just about identical. Brand stories are commercially useful because they are relatively cheap ways to make one product or brand seem different to another.

But creating a brand story poses real challenges. The proliferation of communications channels means that, in the case of a corporation at least, employees, customers and indeed other interested parties can easily add to, and influence, the conversation about the brand. Control is dissipated. This means that it is important that everyone within the company – and ideally outside it too – has a shared vision of what the company is for, why it exists, what it sells and why it is the best choice. A great brand story provides a memorable teaching tool to inspire and guide all stakeholders, and especially to give employees clear cues on how to behave towards customers and each other.

Today you can employ story 'specialists' who will develop the narrative for your company and adapt it for different audiences, including employees, customers, shareholders and investors. This overarching narrative influences the enterprise's larger choices across advertising, sponsorship, product design and staff engagement programs. It becomes a holistic endeavour, embracing the entire enterprise. It may even be embodied at the highest level in mission and vision statements that are signed off by the board.

And there's scientific evidence that stories work. Today even the most sceptical corporate number-crunchers (the accountants and finance types) can't deny that recent neuroscience research verifies the selling power of story. We humans are hardwired for it and our brains use stories – and even invent stories – as a way to process, connect, understand and remember life's events. What's more, even the most compelling numbers and statistics and diagrams can't tell a story by themselves. They require explanation, illumination and context. If there isn't a plausible story produced by the organisation about what the numbers mean, and why they matter, and what that tells us about the direction of the business, then the analysts and shareholders and media will simply invent a story about the numbers for themselves. That usually doesn't end well.

It is something of a mixed blessing that there are more people around the business who have a stake in the leader's speech as part of (or indeed, leading) the broader 'narrative' and want to give helpful suggestions to the speechwriter about what should go into it. It's great that more people recognise the power of story. But too many people blather about narrative without understanding deeply what that really means.

For example, speechwriters and communicators may be told that they need to find a 'new narrative' for the business, when a totally new narrative is unnecessary, unrealistic and undesirable. The fact is that most companies don't want or need a whole new story. What they do want is to keep the great bits of the existing story and minimise the elements that are no longer useful (the perceptions of habitual product failure, the terrible service, the telephone queues). What may be required, therefore, is a revised or updated narrative that feels true to the best beliefs, impulses and achievements of the past.

Often people equate storytelling with simple anecdotes that press emotional buttons. We see this in politics more and more. A broad policy rationale is reduced to a touching personal experience ('I support this veterans' policy because of my grandfather's war experience') or a vignette about a moving individual case ('I support this disability policy because I've just met brave Jane in her wheelchair').

I was once approached by a barrister, working in Public Prosecutions, who asked me to help him create more 'emotional' stories to open and close his speeches to juries. Now, I may be a law school dropout, but I'm fairly sure that the integrity of our legal system relies upon minimising juror bias and striving for fairness and impartiality. I declined that particular opportunity.

Communications experts might imagine that their political or corporate enterprise has a coherent narrative across all its communications channels, when all it has are a bunch of slogans. Like 'Better Schools!' 'A New Way!' 'Real Solutions!' The fact that the outcome may be a moral good (for who doesn't want better schools, new ways or real solutions?) is treated as sufficient policy justification in itself, negating the requirement for explanation of the rationale, approach, cost, risk management, timetable and milestones.

Once I was called in to write a speech for the CEO of a top-10 Australian company with an important enabling role in nearly every aspect of Australian life. The head of marketing at that time was also the head of communications (sometimes this alignment of roles works well, often not), and as the discussion got underway, she told me excitedly about the wonders of the company's big new marketing campaign that was sure to move and excite their customers.

'I know!' she said suddenly. 'Why don't you insert our new tag line into the speech?'

Given that the tag line was something like 'It's Incredible!' I did my best to ignore this advice, and I certainly never inserted a short-term advertising slogan into the leader's speech. That would be to profoundly misunderstand the leader's role, and undermine the leader's reputation.

Sometimes leaders, in a flush of self-admiration, get carried away by the notion that modern leadership is about personal authenticity. I've come across numerous leadership coaches and communication gurus who will charge large sums of money to liberate CEOs from those pesky logical arguments, because they get in the way of what a speech is really all about, which (according to these coaches and gurus) is the speaker's unique passion, values, and real self. Clients then tell me they want their speech to have stories with *passion*, as if passion were an ornament that you could paste on any old speech draft, rather than the intellectual energy driving and shaping it.

Vivid anecdotes and a strong performance style can undoubtedly add weight and colour to a speech. But used at the expense of good argument, they are no better than the anti-intellectual approach favoured by travelling evangelists and self-help gurus. The emotions never last. They fizzle out, or convert to electoral or consumer anger when the implied promises aren't kept.

The leader as chief storyteller

The best leaders tell stories about the group. They speak from the higher vantage point I described earlier. Whether it's the nation. The club. The city. The tribe. Even, the economy. References to their own personal experiences or those of other individuals will only arise as examples within a larger persuasive narrative. The best storytelling engages hearts because it inspires minds.

And remember this: people investing their money like to judge on the past, but they buy on the future. They make a judgement about where the enterprise is headed, which is ultimately a judgement about strategy. And what does strategy consist of but a story about how we will get to a better future? Where we all live (more or less) happily ever after?

This plays to the leader's role and the leader's strengths. A leader's primary job is to take the team from the past to the future. A leader's speech must always connect past and present in such a way as to engender confidence about where the team is headed and how they are getting there. During times of great change, a leader may want to emphasise the reassuring continuities with the past. When there's a revolution underway, the leader may wish to present radical change as an inevitable and natural evolution from previous endeavours. When not much is happening, a leader may want to emphasise previous and present examples of innovation and dynamism.

The speechwriter will, of course, always be mindful that the leader's speech is not some unsigned, disembodied piece of corporate communication. The leader brings their own personality and *ethos* to the cause and has a very particular role to play in advancing it. The leader's story, too, will eventually become part of the larger story of the business, influencing and shaping the brand. But it's not just about them.

In every speech, I make it my business to push the story towards the future with its better company, or country, or way of life.

Sources of inspiration: history, people, world

In order to construct this story of the future, we need to have the right raw materials. I search for these within the history, people and world of the enterprise.

The first source is history. I'm always looking for events in the far or recent past that will illuminate or justify what's happening today, and suggest how this can be built upon to make a better future. While most leaders understandably don't want to use conflict or danger to describe their present circumstances, far-distant history is a safe place to go to for the old mythic tropes like heroic risk and brave overcoming.

Once I came across an incident early on in a company's life when its founders bid for, and won, a contract that was ambitious, given the minuscule scale of the business at that time. The only information I had about this was a few dull lines in a corporate history, but I was able to rework them into a tale of little-guy ambition and unlikely triumph. I then used this anecdote to explain why the company had the confidence to take such bold steps today and why it could confidently expect to succeed: such daring was in the company's DNA.

Another time, I took a few lines from a company history about a long-gone CEO who took a huge risk and personally lobbied (nagged, begged) the then prime minister to change a government decision that seemed likely to badly affect the company's business. Through this CEO's persistence, he eventually changed the prime minister's mind and the course of the company's history. I expanded this into a somewhat heroic but mostly funny tale of determined persuasion and never giving up.

A writer I know worked on a corporate history of a small but hugely successful Australian window company. She discovered that after World War II the owner went to New York City to see the latest developments in aluminium windows. More importantly, she noticed, as a small sideline in her research, that the owner had visited the US company that had provided the technically innovative external walls, made of glass, for the modernist new United Nations building in New York. This was too good an opportunity to miss. She wrote that surely the Australian leader would have stood before the marvellous new building with its soaring windows, symbolic of a brave new world, and dreamed of new ideas to be taken back to Australia. An inspirational image and a great way to advance the modern story of this forward-thinking Australian business. All this narrative goodness obtained from a brief aside in an old company history.

The second clear source for story is the people of the company. The micro-story of one individual worker or a hardworking team can be immensely powerful, which is why many smart companies use their employees as their spokespeople. Long-time front-line employees are usually the best sources of great yarns. The speechwriter is often in a unique position to meander around (unthreateningly, for we have little or no institutional power) and hear about the company from these workers who know it best – not the spin version of the business, but the reality of its day-to-day operations. Many will share their tales about the time they worked day and night to solve a crisis, or went out of their way to help a customer in trouble, or threw the world's greatest party when they won a big deal. In the previous chapter we saw how Walmart employee Jessica Lewis exemplified the best traditions of Walmart culture through her practical assistance for the victims of Hurricane Katrina.

Strangely, it takes a lot more work for the speechwriter to coax rich stories from middle managers. They know the business intimately but are wary of venturing anywhere near office politics; have been trained into caution to protect their promotion prospects; and the strict hierarchy of most corporations encourages only the most succinct, outcome-focused answers by the middle ranks in work meetings. So the challenge, when soliciting a middle manager's input into a speech on any subject, is not that they will bang on about their workplace lows and highs but, on the contrary, that they will merely provide a brisk three-line summary.

For a different reason, the same applies when soliciting information from company experts about technical matters. The expert will generally give the speechwriter a short overview of the new system or technology, assuming she won't be capable of understanding the complexity of the detail. It's true the speechwriter is looking for the humanity in the story, but that will only emerge when she understands how people have wrangled tough technical issues and business problems. Often the speechwriter needs to become very knowledgeable herself so she can own and shape the lines properly. This means that laziness for a speechwriter is not an option. If it involves finding out the details of the supply chain or the production line or the new technology, and deeply understanding the processes and benefits, then so be it. That's how you make a narrative rich.

The third source of inspiration is the 'world' of the enterprise. Not long ago, I was introduced to a successful film and TV producer at a friend's lunch. We spoke about his various productions and what he was planning to do next. This teller of thrilling stories said not a word to me about storytelling or narrative. Instead, he said, 'In a long-running series, what we are really looking for is a rich world that people want to enter and return to.' A rich world. Of course. Think about why you love *Game of Thrones*, or *Mad Men* or, as in my case, *The West Wing*. Isn't it the case that you love the show because you love the world it inhabits? I will watch even an inferior episode of a favourite show and still enjoy it, simply because I feel at home in that particular world. People don't watch *Frasier* re-runs for something new: we watch these programs precisely because they offer a familiar, comforting place to return to. Isn't that what every enterprise aspires to be: a long-running and beloved 'hit series'? That's why Qantas evokes 'home' and the NRMA reminds us of security.

The success of so-called franchise movies can also be attributed to the pleasure of familiarity with a particular world. If I think of James Bond, I can immediately list a bunch of Bond-ish world elements: beautiful girls, an Aston Martin, a martini, the famous opening titles, global locations, London, M and Q and Miss Moneypenny, and an uber-villain with a quirk.

Now think of powerful brands like Apple, or Chanel, or Ikea. If I think of those brands, I also conjure up a mix of images and feelings that amount to a particular 'world'. With Apple, it's the products and their common features that I imagine: elegance, simplicity, ease of use, a feeling of being plugged into ultra-modernity and endless creative potential. Chanel means iconic pieces like tweed jackets, little black dresses, quilted handbags and camellias, a feeling of glamour linked to heritage. Ikea really is a visible world: the world of the giant Ikea shop and the pleasures of budget homemaking.

So consider the world of the enterprise itself. What are the defining elements of that world? What makes it special? What sets it apart? How do you feel when you are in that world? Secure? Excited? Rewarded? Safe? The leader could mention some large or small detail about that world then link it to the bigger corporate picture. Details may include items as simple as:

· The vibrant logo, designed to convey a spirit of optimism.
· The sturdy uniforms that mean staff can focus on comfort and customers.
· The signature welcome 'hello' when customers call.
· The way the 'on' button is placed on the latest model for ease of use.

These little inconsequential details can easily be overlooked as parts of the corporate narrative. But by specifically recalling them in speeches, and linking them to the larger strategy, leaders can renew that sense of pleasure and connection that people have with their world, even if it's not populated by superheroes but is just a consumer goods company, a bank or a telecommunications service.

It's also instructive to think of the things that *can't* happen in a particular world, because that helps to define the world even more clearly. James Bond as an uncle of three adorable children? *Nah.* James Bond with an unsightly cold sore? *Nope.* How about James Bond opening a corner store? *I don't think so.*

In much the same way we might ask: should a bank ever sponsor a boxing competition? That would never work. But when optometry and eye-ware firm OPSM sponsors AFL umpires, whose performance relies upon spotting the details of a fast-moving game, well, that's nothing short of genius.

As a speechwriter, for me it's a joy to assemble all this great story material. It's like having a fridge, freezer and pantry stocked with good ingredients: you always have the makings of a good meal.

The leader's double perspective: thinking with feeling

My friend the novelist Charlotte Wood tells me that when we talk about the hunger for stories, what we are really hungry for is *meaning.* Yes, the history, people and world of the enterprise provide good raw material. But only the synthesis of reason and emotion will infuse that raw material with a larger meaning. We want true nourishment from our leaders, not just a brief sugary high.

To understand this idea further we can look to the thoughtful observations of Phillip Lopate, the world's pre-eminent teacher of the art of personal memoir. In his book *To Show and to Tell* (2013), Lopate proposes that innocence, naïveté and sentimentality have no place in this genre, and that all the heated passions and messy emotions of experience must be mediated in memoirs by analysis, judgement and worldly appraisal. Sounds like leadership to me. Lopate argues the need for a 'double perspective', in which authors makes use of intellectual hindsight to illuminate, consider and reflect upon their experiences.

Lopate's point on memoirs holds equally true for leadership speeches. After all, as he puts it:

> *... emotion and thinking are not mutually exclusive,*
> *but can coexist: passionately argued thought can have*
> *affective warmth, just as feelings can be thoughtfully and*
> *delicately parsed.*

We need our politicians and business leaders to be rational, pragmatic and far-sighted. We need them to be more articulate and informed than we are. We need them *to know better*, in a profound sense. And most of all, we need them to be ready to defend and advance their case through careful argumentation, along with appeals to emotion.

We all crave these true, fact-based stories that make sense of our world; that help us understand where we are going and how we will get there. But that doesn't mean simply replacing clear lines of thought or argument with one or more colourful personal anecdotes. It's harder and better than that. It means mind and heart coming together.

Case study

The moving power of facts: former President
Bill Clinton versus President Barack Obama in 2012

At the Democratic Convention of 2012, former US President Bill Clinton had the honour of introducing the incumbent President (and presidential candidate) Barack Obama. This was a 45-minute speech about the dry subject of the American economy but it managed to have loads of heart. The speech was punctuated by roars of audience laughter, loud applause, standing ovations, boos for the enemy and cheers for Obama. What was everyone inspired by? Facts, told with verve, humour and passion. Facts, told in detail and with proof. Facts, and the way those facts were drawn together in a reasoned way to create a bigger picture, a compelling story of America's recent past and potentially better future.

Let's look at just one brief section near the top of the speech, as Clinton put forward a high-level argument for President Obama's re-election in front of the large assembly of Democrat true believers, and beyond that, a no doubt far more sceptical national TV audience:

> *Here it is. He inherited a deeply damaged economy. He put a floor under the crash. He began the long hard road to recovery and laid the foundation for a modern, more well-balanced economy that will produce millions of good new jobs, vibrant new businesses and lots of new wealth for innovators.*

It was clearly a positive economic story. But no story is complete without its trials, and no speech works without the truth. So then Clinton quite explicitly pointed out the great big elephant in the room:

Now, are we where we want to be today? No. Is the President satisfied? Of course not.

Next he circled back again:

But are we better off than we were when he took office?

The audience cheered, 'YES!' Already Clinton was wagging his finger, rocking back and forth, face glowing pinkly. The story was underway.

And listen to this. Listen to this, everybody ... When President Obama took office, the economy was in free fall. It had just shrunk 9 full per cent of GDP. We were losing 750,000 jobs a month. Are we doing better than that today?

'YES!' cheered the audience.

Now, look. Here's the challenge he faces and the challenge all of you who support him face. I get it. I know it. I've been there. A lot of Americans are still angry and frustrated about this economy. If you look at the numbers, employment is growing, banks are beginning to lend again. And in a lot of places, housing prices are even beginning to pick up.

Still, though, he was not finished with the bad news. His emphatic tone was softened by the soft southern voice and the confiding half-smile:

But too many people do not feel it yet.

We can now sense that Clinton was cranking up. Having acknowledged how bad things seemed to be, he would have to persuade this audience to believe that things were going to improve.

Clinton could have chosen to travel an emotive path and talk about his faith in the President, or his belief in the awesome regenerative power of the United States. But he chose not to go down that road of faith or belief or some other emotion. Instead, he searched for some form of proof. And in the absence of clear data about the future, he advanced a plausible analogy (an analogy with the happy side benefit of reminding the audience of his own achievements in office):

I had the same thing happen in 1994 and early '95. We could see that the policies were working, that the economy was growing. But most people didn't feel it yet, and we were halfway through the longest peacetime expansion in the history of the United States.

169

Applause from the audience. And he went on:

But, wait, wait.

Again, the tilting finger, the rosy cheeks, the coaxing voice, the half-smile:

The difference this time is purely in the circumstances. President Obama started with a much weaker economy than I did. Listen to me, now. No President – no President – not me, not any of my predecessors, no one could have fully repaired all the damage that he found in just four years. Now, he has laid the foundation for a new modern successful economy of shared prosperity. And if you will renew the President's contract, you will feel it. You will feel it ...

This is stirring, passionate stuff. 'You will feel it ... you will feel it ...' But Clinton didn't want to dwell too long on the emotions, because he needed to bring the audience back to the main point:

So let's get back to the story. In 2010 as the President's Recovery Program kicked in, the job losses stopped and things began to turn around. The Recovery Act saved or created millions of jobs and cut taxes – let me say this again – cut taxes for 95 per cent of the American people. And in the last 29 months, our economy has produced about four-and-a-half million jobs.

He paused, because he'd nailed a key fact. Then:

So here's another jobs score. President Obama: plus four-and-a-half million. Congressional Republicans: zero.

The audience shouted and applauded.

Note how Clinton kept telling the audience to calm down, to 'listen', 'look', 'pay attention', 'wait'. He wasn't after the swelling admiration and applause, he was after careful attention. Like a schoolteacher shushing his excitable pupils, he had an urgent need to get a few facts into their brains before the class ended.

Clinton carried on from here, giving more detail on the President's key initiatives, which would serve to build the strong national economy he'd been foreshadowing. He explained the President's policies on healthcare, student loans, automotive jobs, energy, debt management. He didn't just declare the merits of each policy, he set out its rationale, how it was working and what it would achieve, and provided key numbers to back up his assertions. Along the way, he exposed the logical flaws and weaknesses in the Republican Party's case against Obama, and in its case for its own presidential candidate.

President Clinton was telling a story of a national economy that was emerging, bumpily but surely, from its low point; an economy whose positive indicators preceded improvements on the ground; an economy whose prospects were immeasurably strengthened by the quality of the leader at the helm and the policy approaches he championed. It's the speech of a policy wonk, the kind that is increasingly unfashionable, because to develop a speech like this requires the capacity to know, distil and explain complex ideas.

As journalist John Heilemann beautifully put it in *New York Magazine*, in this speech, Clinton achieved 'a quartet of objectives: distillation, litigation, validation and evisceration' in the manner of 'an aw-shucks southern country lawyer (albeit one with a public-policy PhD)'.

The Clinton speech was so well received that it overshadowed the subsequent Obama speech, which was, in any case, most atypically flat – lacking, as Heilemann noted, his usual 'soaring stanzas and almost preacherly cadences'.

In comparison with Clinton's, Obama's speech was notable for its use of emotional hooks. In speaking of Medicare, Obama referred to 'a little girl with a heart disorder in Phoenix'. On student loans, he mentioned a 'young man in Colorado who never thought he'd be able to afford his dream of earning a medical degree'. On the American Dream, he referred to 'the young woman I met at a science fair who won national recognition for her biology research while living with her family at a homeless shelter'. Compelling vignettes, but if you are a die-hard Democrat looking to proselytise the President's cause, what can you do with these stories? You can't retail those Obama anecdotes as your own; you can't adopt them as *your* persuasive argument for his re-election.

The Clinton story, on the other hand, is definitely one that that you could use in discussions with your neighbour, or your work colleague, or your sceptical aunty. 'Sure,' you could say lightly, when they tell you that things are junk under this administration, 'things don't feel better yet, but remember, the same thing happened back in the '90s ... and we got out of that one. And guess how many jobs have been created in just over two years?'

Clinton's speech is a fine example of the practice that Australian Prime Minister Gough Whitlam encouraged his speechwriter Graham Freudenberg to adopt. As far as Gough Whitlam was concerned, wrote Freudenberg, 'His standing instruction and his standard complaint to people preparing speech material for him is "More matter and less art".' Because it's out of the matter that you create the art.

Case study

Striking the balance: the case of TED Talks

It is impossible to talk about modern speechmaking without including the TED Talks, those speeches distributed freely online under the slogan 'Ideas Worth Spreading'. I think they're great. I have watched and enjoyed and learned valuable things from any number of them.

When we think about the interplay of stories, reason and emotion in modern oratory, the trajectory of the TED Talks is instructive. When TED started out in the 1980s, its speakers were the nerds, geeks and techies of the entertainment, technology and design industries. The aim was to get these uncommunicative experts to share their specialised knowledge with each other, and thereby to encourage greater innovation and collaboration across fields of knowledge. To make the bridge work, the TED organisers coached these largely introverted experts to address just one important idea, within a strict time limit of 18 minutes. They were to bring their subject to life by using the power of story, and by connecting their own passion to the topic. The aim was to use storytelling not for its own sake, but for the sake of improving the pool of knowledge.

As the TED phenomenon snowballed, the most popular talks generated what is known as 'contagious emotion', and were widely circulated and viewed online. But then came the problem. Speakers came to obsess over the number of online likes and hits they received. They would fall apart if their delivered speeches didn't get an overwhelmingly positive response. They started going for the cheap emotional hit, looking for short-term praise over long-term impact.

The TED people are smart, and good at learning as they go. Today the coaches from TED, while still encouraging speakers to follow the same basic speech preparation guidelines, remind speakers that they should not focus only on passion or purely on feeling, but also stick with the core mission of communicating an exciting and challenging idea. So even the TED industry has had to regulate the surge towards emotional overload.

One of the more exhilarating TED Talks was delivered under the TEDx Program, a community-run offshoot of TED. It was delivered by Californian academic Benjamin H Bratton in 2013, and was, incidentally, a demonstration by TED of an admirable commitment to freedom of speech. The speech was titled 'What's Wrong with TED Talks?' and was critical of the entire TED enterprise, which Bratton argued was dumbing down hard issues by focusing on the 'personal journey of insight and realisation' rather than dealing with challenges facing the world that are 'complicated and difficult and not given to tidy just-so solutions'.

It was a cracking speech, and I take Bratton's point. His remarks highlight TED's limitations in format and content. A brilliant and accomplished acquaintance of mine has given both a TEDx Talk and a full-blown TED Talk, and she agrees that there are frustrations in the process. When preparing her talks she felt there were pressures on her to make them a bit too relentlessly upbeat. She was so over-rehearsed she wondered if some of the energy had gone from her speeches before she'd even given them. Most of all, she told me, it required months of work and sweat and effort and grind to get the speeches just right, according to the standards of the TED editors, and she would be reluctant to make that level of investment ever again. (Of course, this was also an indication of the effort that really does need to go into delivering good speeches.) At the same time, she gladly conceded that the global exposure given to her ideas had changed her life, and led to opportunities to speak in very senior business and academic forums where she could finally say what she wanted, in the detail she wanted and in the manner that made her feel most comfortable.

Certainly, as Bratton noted, TED Talks can overemphasise the personal journey at the expense of the powerfully reasoned argument. However, it is now clear that TED has recognised this fault and is addressing it, trying to redirect the focus towards that central 'Idea Worth Spreading'.

I am less interested in what TED *can't* do than what TED is actually achieving. Those online talks are an effective – if simplified – way to discover the modern world's interesting thinkers. The rigorous TED guidelines ensure there is no pompous oratory, no longwinded jargon, no gimmicks. TED presents us with the joy of human minds engaging with ideas. Delivering a TED Talk can give a speaker political influence, attract investors and backers, win research grants, get book contracts.

Looking ahead, I think we will find that TED has raised our expectations about what we should expect from speeches. Corporate leaders will need to lift their game. Even the dullest central banker will be compelled to improve their public presentations. As it evolves, TED may represent the bright future of rhetoric.

Unleashing the power of ceremonial speeches

The CEO diary may not appear to offer a great many opportunities to tell rich and fulfilling stories that nourish hearts and minds. But that is to ignore the most under-rated speech type of all – the ceremonial speech.

I used to think I was the only person who straightened up in delighted anticipation when the time came around for speeches at parties and weddings. Everyone else seemed to slump and quietly slink towards the bar. But time has vindicated my enthusiasm. Even as conventional religious rituals have progressively faded, in private life there are more ceremonies, and ceremonial speeches, than ever. People now construct elaborate secular rituals, not just around births, deaths and marriages, but also around milestone birthdays and wedding anniversaries, and even invent new rituals such as 'divorce parties' and 'gender reveals'.

It is no coincidence that these occasions invariably include what are known as ceremonial speeches. It certainly comes as no surprise to me. Many of us live in a lonely and godless world, and we hunger for ceremonies that lend significance to our days. I am routinely asked to help out with speeches for ritual events, and I love doing so. They reflect a longing for meaning that I share.

One of the great myths about ceremonies is that they are occasions in which people come together as a united group. Not really. In fact, few occasions reveal deep, underlying divisions and discord more than a ceremonial event. The family feuds. The grievances of one faction or another. The envy and resentments of the losers. The task of the speaker, therefore, becomes a complex and almost priestly one. They must find a way to both acknowledge and, if required, rise above all the different opinions and feelings that will be in play.

A very nice English businessman, the highly successful eldest brother in a group of disparate siblings, contacted me in some distress when his mother died. He was to make the family speech at the funeral, but it was complicated. He had had a happy relationship with his mother. He was keen to honour her, without overlooking her considerable (if loveable) foibles, or the fact that some of his siblings had mixed feelings about her. And when I say mixed, I mean that even in adulthood they were unable to let go of their anger about her lax mothering style and irrational devotion to her dogs.

The two of us talked about this problem for a long while over several rather emotional phone calls. In the end, this is the gist of what we wrote:

She was an unusual mother in many ways, and we, her children, will each have our own memories of her. Some of us certainly wished she were more conventional. What I remember is ...

And so it went on. The eldest son rang me in a state of relief after the funeral to say that he felt he had paid proper, loving tribute to his mother, he had spoken the truth, and his siblings didn't resent him.

Another time I worked on a milestone birthday speech to be delivered by the birthday boy, the ebullient head of a large family company. The celebration was to be big and lavish. He told me that he wanted to say to his dad (and I am only barely paraphrasing here), 'Dad, if only you'd bought your first block of units in the city instead of that regional backwater, we could all be a lot richer today.' And he thought he might tell his brother, 'You're pretty much a waste of space and a lazy do-nothing, but I luvsya anyway.' To his wife, he was keen to say, 'You are over-controlling and you've never given me a moment's peace, but you are a fantastic mother.' He was clearly dismayed by the somewhat watery alternatives I offered to those uncompromising remarks, and I suspect he opted for his own more direct version on the day. It must have been quite a party.

Richard Curtis is a British film director and writer who has a powerful understanding of the role of ritual and ceremony in our lives. His *Four Weddings and a Funeral* is a film entirely structured around ceremonial speeches. It is very funny, and very romantic, and also poignant in parts. The genius of the film is that all the key scenes occur in connection with ceremonial events (four weddings and a funeral, naturally) – and we watch the characters as they experience their own heightened feelings and sensations as they hope for love, regret love lost, worry about their capacity to love, recognise true love in their midst only as someone dies, and finally identify what true love means. We even have a bonus example of public speaking going wrong with Rowan Atkinson playing a nervous apprentice vicar who can't get his words right. Curtis went on to make *Love, Actually*, which is an ensemble story linked by the rituals of Christmas, and it famously begins and ends with footage of the ritual reunions of families and lovers at the arrivals terminal of Heathrow Airport.

Modern public ceremonial speeches take many forms. Speeches are still an important part of military and veterans' events such as ANZAC Day in Australia and Memorial Day in the United States. Then there are graduation or commencement addresses, and the presenting or accepting of awards at sporting, creative arts and academic competitions and many other occasions. As I mentioned earlier, some of the most popular speeches online today are inspirational commencement speeches by eminent business and cultural figures.

The modern era has many downsides, but one of the great things about it is the way people are far more comfortable with sharing their true selves. When my brother and his wife got married, I discovered how buttoned-up I was as I heard them talking quite openly in their wedding speeches about the terms they had agreed on for their marriage. It wasn't that they were shocking terms; quite the contrary. They were funny and real and full of knowledge about each other's pasts and eccentricities. We don't have to pretend we are late Victorians any more, and that makes for far more powerful speeches.

A favourite speech of mine is Earl Spencer's speech at the funeral of his sister Diana, Princess of Wales in 1997, in which he attacked the paparazzi directly and the royal family indirectly. But some of the most powerful lines lovingly confront the elephant in the room of Diana's unstable personality:

> For all the status, the glamour, the applause, Diana
> remained throughout a very insecure person at heart,
> almost childlike in her desire to do good for others so she
> could release herself from deep feelings of unworthiness
> of which her eating disorders were merely a symptom.
> The world sensed this part of her character and cherished her
> for her vulnerability whilst admiring her for her honesty.

Some of the speeches we remember best are, in fact, ceremonial speeches. The most famous speech in antiquity was Pericles's speech to democratic Athens in 431 BCE, in honour of the city's war dead:

> *Realize for yourself the power of Athens, and feed your eyes upon her day after day, till you become her devoted lover. Then, when all her greatness breaks upon you, reflect that it was by courage, sense of duty and a keen feeling of honor in action that men were enabled to win all this, and that no personal failure in an enterprise could make them consent to deprive their country of their valor, but they laid it at her feet as the most glorious contribution they could offer. By this mutual offering of their lives made by them all, they each of them individually received that renown which never grows old. For a sepulchre they have won not so much that tomb in which their bones are here deposited, but that noblest of shrines wherein their glory is laid up to be eternally remembered upon every occasion on which deed or story shall fall for its commemoration. For heroes have the whole earth for their tomb.*

Abraham Lincoln's Gettysburg Address was also a speech in honour of the dead, and you can hear the rhythms and echoes of Pericles in these words, although shaped to sorrow instead of glory:

... we can not dedicate, we can not consecrate, we can not hallow – this ground. The brave men, living and dead, who struggled here, have consecrated it, far above our poor power to add or detract. The world will little note, nor long remember what we say here, but it can never forget what they did here. It is for us the living, rather, to be dedicated here to the unfinished work which they who fought here have thus far so nobly advanced.

One of Australia's greatest speeches was delivered by Prime Minister Paul Keating on Remembrance Day 1993 at the Tomb of the Unknown Soldier in Canberra (another Don Watson speech). Read the lines aloud and you will hear the beautiful weight and balance of the sentences:

This Unknown Australian is not interred here to glorify war over peace; or to assert a soldier's character above a civilian's; or one race or one nation or one religion above another; or men above women; or the war in which he fought and died above any other war; or of one generation above any that has or will come later. The Unknown Soldier honours the memory of all those men and women who laid down their lives for Australia. His tomb is a reminder of what we have lost in war and what we have gained.

A softer strand of leadership

Ceremonial speeches make up a significant part of any CEO's diary, from retirement parties to staff awards nights to the opening of a new wing and milestone company anniversaries. But the curious thing is this: despite their clear importance to the way our communities work, ceremonial speeches are very seriously underutilised as opportunities to demonstrate leadership.

A great ceremonial speech can, like no other, do important things for a leader. Create a new shade in their public persona. Advance, as if by stealth, the speaker's broader agenda. Take an audience to a deeper place. Ceremonial speeches provide a rare opportunity for leaders to use, without irony, the great words – words like 'courage', 'honour', 'frankness', 'friendship' and even 'love'. And they can also provide an opportunity to deliver difficult messages.

But, as I've seen many times, the honour of preparing the ceremonial speech is often passed down to the most junior person and left to the last minute. I guess the rationale behind this is that the risk is fairly low and the job can be trusted to a speechwriter-in-training. But that is to ignore the massive opportunity offered by the ceremonial speech. It also ignores how hard such a speech is to write. The speechwriter sits with a vacant mind before a blank screen. There is nothing new to say, nothing to announce or denounce, and no crisis. Where to start? Certainly the speech can draw for raw content upon the sources of inspiration I set out in Chapter 4: the history, people and world of the enterprise or cause.

Perhaps it is even more important to have the right frame of mind when crafting a ceremonial speech. A ceremonial speech is about what binds us together as a community. It reminds us why we love each other despite our flaws, and stick together despite our differences, and remember our stories, and keep to our traditions and fight for our shared beliefs.

The ceremonial speech is about who we are, where we are from, and what we may become. Franz Kafka famously called the novel 'an axe for the frozen sea within us'. Great ceremonial speeches are an axe for the frozen sea *between* us.

Case study

Finding the right tone: PepsiCo CEO Indra Nooyi in 2005 and 2015

In 2005, Indra Nooyi, then Chief Financial Officer of PepsiCo worldwide, addressed the graduating class of Columbia University Business School in New York City. She would no doubt have been warmly received. After all, she was an exceptional example of the potency of the American dream. Nooyi was born in India and graduated from the Indian Institute of Management in Calcutta before going on to Yale University for her second MBA. She had a stint at a management consulting firm, then commenced the stellar career at PepsiCo that has made her one of the world's best-known business leaders and a role model for professional women.

Nooyi is an eloquent communicator, and at Columbia University Business School she would have encountered an audience of young, ambitious people who must have seemed very familiar to her, like younger versions of herself. I'm sure she would have felt confident that she could deliver a stirring and even challenging address on broad-mindedness and the need for a global outlook to this sophisticated and sympathetic audience. But things went astray.

Nooyi took an audacious approach and decided to build her speech around an image, creating an analogy in which the five fingers of the hand represented the five major continents of the world (thus excluding Australia altogether, as it happens). And then she pushed her luck and suggested that America was the world's middle finger, adding, 'it really stands out ... if used inappropriately – just like the US itself – the middle finger can convey a negative message and get us in trouble. You know what I'm talking about. Unfortunately, I think this is how the rest of the world looks at the US right now.'

Then she gave force to her point through an anecdote about five Americans in a bar in China who ridiculed the 'hotel's lavatory facilities' in loud English and were oblivious to the fact that their Chinese hosts spoke English and understood every word.

Nooyi was clearly sensitive to the provocative nature of these remarks, and emphasised that this critique of America stemmed from a place of love:

Graduates, it pains me greatly that this view of America persists. Although I'm a daughter of India, I'm an American businesswoman. My family and I are citizens of this great country. This land we call home is a most

*loving and ever-giving nation – a Promised Land that we
love dearly in return. And it represents a true force that,
if used for good, can steady the hand – along with global
economies and cultures.*

But these last conciliatory words, this celebration of shared
patriotism, couldn't undo the damage of the previous
paragraphs. The speech must have come across to her
audience as a judgement of American ways, if not altogether
anti-American. When Nooyi's 'America as the middle finger'
remarks became public, there were calls for a boycott of Pepsi
products, and Nooyi posted an apology on the PepsiCo website.

Nooyi is a tough and canny operator, and knows how to
learn a lesson. Ten years later, in April 2015, then the chair
and CEO of PepsiCo, she delivered another graduation address,
this time to students at the Indian Institute of Management
in Calcutta, her old *alma mater.* By this time she had become
more skilled at delivering tough messages in soft ways.

Nooyi's 2015 speech began conventionally enough, with a
humorous anecdote, warm congratulations to the students, and
kind remarks to the parents sitting in the rows behind them.
Nooyi then reminisced about her own days at the Institute of
Management, when India was a far more inward, undeveloped
place. Without saying so directly, she implied that as an
ambitious woman in the modern world, she had no choice but
to leave India to make her career. She then moved on to detail
all the positive developments that had taken place in India over
the intervening 40 years, chronicling the country's emergence

as the world's fastest-growing free-market economy and a hub of technological innovation. As she said, 'It's safe to say you are all headed for wildly successful careers.' She went on:

So I'm not here to tell you how to have a successful career. I'm here to tell you that a successful career is not enough. With the many blessings you have received, with the world-class education you have just completed, with all the incredible resources available to you right here in India, you must make something more.

She was getting it just right here. She was setting herself up to give the Indian graduates a message that was almost as tough as the one she'd given to the Columbia graduates, but this time using exhortation and inspiration as her levers, rather than criticism. Now she came to the tough core message:

As much progress as India and the world have made over the last four decades, we still have a long way to go. We still face complex challenges – like inequality, climate change and resource scarcity – that demand solutions and leadership.

At the same time, no issue can be contained within a particular country. Most issues you will deal with are global. You will have to learn how to take off your blinkers, think expansively, and realize that you are part of a global ecosystem. It is critical that you take this responsibility seriously, because you are the problem-

*solvers and leaders we need to overcome our world's most
serious challenges ... I'm confident that you will show up.*

'You will have to learn how to take off your blinkers.' It was
exactly the same call to a global mindset that Nooyi delivered
to this audience's American peers 10 years earlier, but told
in such a careful and nuanced way that this time it became
a powerful argument for global corporate citizenship. Nooyi
ensured that she did not come across as an American woman
(and a woman who had left India behind) hectoring Indians
on their problems and duties, but rather as a thoughtful leader
with a positive and inspirational message. The speech reflected
a far more sophisticated understanding of how to convey a
challenging message without causing offence.

I wonder whether it was also designed to correct, once and
for all, any lingering perception left by the 2005 speech that
Nooyi was un-American. Because it demonstrated that she was
prepared to serve tough love both to her country of origin and
to her adopted home.

The tale of Nooyi's two speeches is a reminder of the delicacy
and sensitivity of the ceremonial speech, and the impact it can
have on the leader's reputation, both positive and negative.

Inspiring a ceremonial audience

Ceremonial speeches are not like most other speeches in public
life. If you go to an ordinary business lunch, for example, the
audience will be busy, diverse and half-preoccupied by other
matters as the speech begins. On those occasions the speaker's

challenge is to generate interest and emotion around the room. When I am drafting business speeches, I have a sense that if I get it right, energy will be created in the room as the speech is delivered. But with ceremonial speeches, it's a very different process. The energy is already there in the room, though it may be muted and undeveloped. The job of the speech – the leader's task – is to tap into that energy and reflect it back to the audience, in whom it will swell and magnify. The speech becomes a form of communion.

If the leader or their team has anything to do with planning the event, I always recommend that the leader deliver the speech as early as possible. The speech therefore plays the role of binding together all the people attending the event. It reminds them what they care about in common, and what they share. And it makes the rest of the event far more rich and meaningful, because even if the guests don't know each other at first, they will be able to relate to each other via the shared emotions and memories arising from the speech.

I divide the audiences for ceremonial speeches into four main categories:

1. People who have come together because they all love, honour or respect the same person – such as at weddings, birthdays and funerals.

2. People who have gathered to express shared fundamental values – such as at religious services or social rallies.

3. People who work for the same cause – whether it is a political objective, a company or a charity.

4. People who have come together because of a shared experience (whether enjoyed or endured) – perhaps as classmates, teammates or colleagues.

What you realise, when you think about it carefully, is that in each of these categories, the audience will be emotionally engaged. Ceremonial speeches are not straightforward but rather freighted with complex feelings of nostalgia, regret, hope, grief and love. The emotional temperature will be high. Which means there will be more than the usual level of interest in what the speaker has to say, and a yearning for it to be meaningful. Perhaps that is why people sometimes groan in anticipation of the speeches on ceremonial occasions. They're expressing fear and expectation of disappointment.

On any ceremonial occasion, there will almost certainly be one or more people in the audience who *really* matter. It might be the bride, the project manager, the descendants of the founder, the children, the widow or the individual being honoured. The speaker should always find a way to address the people in the room who really care, and who really need to hear what the speaker is going to say. And that works because everyone else in the audience probably cares very much about these people too. That's why Nooyi's 2015 speech in India made special mention of the parents of the graduating class.

Drafting a ceremonial speech for someone else can be difficult.

It can be tricky coaxing from a busy politician or corporate leader what they might want to say at an event that is of little obvious significance. Most of the time they *don't know* what they want to say; their head is full of material problems and they find it hard to focus on something that appears to be a second or third order priority. But have a go and ask the big questions:

· What does this event say to you?
· What is your experience or recollection?

Listen for any key words. Note them and include them in the draft.

Many ceremonial speeches are annual or regular events. But the flux of time and history changes the world of the speech. Read previous years' versions; ask what has changed. Is the world stronger, or sadder? Is life getting harder, or easier? Consider how what's happening today affects our view of both the past and the future.

You only have to watch the Academy Awards to know that even the simplest ceremonial speech needs structure. A list of acknowledgements is not a speech. Package the list and consider what it means. An introduction or a thank you can be a reflection on purpose, on persistence, on teamwork, on overcoming.

At the outset, it is always essential that the leader honour the ceremony. Remind people why they have turned up and why they care. This is when you can reflect and pay tribute to the audience and its mood. Tell people why 'we are gathered here today'. Openly express what they are feeling: 'in sorrow', 'with joy', 'with mixed emotions', 'with fear and hope' or, as I said at my long-time bachelor brother's wedding, 'at last!' Often it is right and proper to recount certain facts for the record. The leader should not hesitate to do so.

The audience will arrive asking, 'Remind me why I'm here?' They will be hoping for a mirror of their emotions from the speech. But they will end up wanting something more. They want to know: 'Where do we go from here?' Your message does not have to be big. But it does need to resonate. Ask yourself: *Is the aim to reinforce existing values, continue to push change, or spark something new and big? Where do we put this revived emotional energy, happy or sad?* That's why it is important to give the audience some relevant emotional action:

- 'As we leave here today, let us be inspired to ...'
- 'Let us dedicate ourselves (or rededicate ourselves) to ...'
- 'Let us ask ourselves how we can further the cause of ...'
- 'Let us go away thankful for ...'
- 'We will always take pride in ...'

Whatever the call to action, it will always arise from something pre-existing, from deep embedded values within the audience itself. There are times of trouble, times of change, times of joy, when something important should be said. It can only be said by the leader, and it can only be said in the form of a speech. It's a sacred human task, and getting the ceremonial language right can create a wave of positive emotion for the speaker. It is also one of the most important opportunities for the speechwriter.

Case study

Redefining Australian leadership:
Indigenous leader Noel Pearson in 2014

Australia's greatest contemporary orator, Aboriginal leader Noel Pearson, delivered one of the best ceremonial speeches of recent times when he gave a eulogy for former Australian prime minister Gough Whitlam at Sydney Town Hall in 2014. Other speakers that day included the actor Cate Blanchett; Whitlam's former speechwriter and confidant Graham Freudenberg; and Antony Whitlam, Gough's eldest son. So it might have been expected, in accordance with the usual polite distribution of oratorical duties, that Pearson would largely confine his remarks to Whitlam's contribution to the advancement of Aboriginal land rights and civil rights.

Pearson did that, but he accomplished so much more: he used a 20-minute speech to suggest an entirely new way for Australians to think about what we want of our leaders, and how we might conceive of ourselves as a nation.

Throughout the speech Pearson referred to Whitlam as 'this old man'. 'Without this old man,' he said, 'the land and human rights of our people would never have seen the light of day.' And again, 'My signal honour today on behalf of more people than I could ever know, is to express our immense gratitude for the public service of this old man.' And, 'The achievements of this old man are present in the institutions we today take for granted and played no small part in the progress of modern Australia.'

How startling this is. In white culture, to speak of a leader as 'this old man' is to consign him to pitiful irrelevance. But Noel Pearson was deploying the phrase out of a very different tradition: he spoke of Gough Whitlam as one might speak of a famous Aboriginal elder, a man whose accumulated wisdom, whose knowledge of tribal lore, whose leadership of his people, warranted the highest honorific. As is customary in the 'welcome to country' ceremonies conducted around Australia, Pearson was paying solemn tribute to the contributions of an elder, now past. This particular elder happened to be white.

But what made this speech so exciting is that there was more: a second fine tradition of leadership that Pearson wove through his words. Gough Whitlam was well known to have started his academic life as a classicist, studying ancient Greek and Latin at Sydney University before switching to the law, always openly delighting in the ancient worlds of Greece and Rome that gave rise to so much that is good in western civilisation. Pearson described, and paid comic tribute to, Whitlam's leadership in this classical tradition when, in the ironic mode adopted by the Monty Python troupe, he asked rhetorically, 'What did this Roman ever do for us?'

He then reminded us:

Apart from Medibank and the Trade Practices Act, cutting tariff protections, no-fault divorce in the Family Law Act, the Australia Council, the Federal Court, the Order of Australia, federal legal aid, the Racial Discrimination Act, needs-based schools funding, the recognition of China, the

abolition of conscription, the Law Reform Commission,
student financial assistance, the Heritage Commission,
non-discriminatory immigration rules, community
health clinics, Aboriginal land rights, paid maternity
leave for public servants, lowering the minimum voting
age to 18 years and fair electoral boundaries and Senate
representation for the territories.

Note the glorious power of a well-written list in a speech. And then Pearson pushed his classical analogy even further with a joyous image of Whitlam in grand senatorial style:

And the Prime Minister with that classical Roman mien,
one who would have been as naturally garbed in a toga as
a safari suit, stands imperiously with twinkling eyes and
that slight self-mocking smile playing around his mouth, in
turn infuriating his enemies and delighting his followers.

Gough Whitlam was a rare individual: a cosmopolitan who could comfortably stroll the ancient Via Sacra in Rome, quoting Cicero in the original, and musing on Julius Caesar's legacy as the High Priest or *Pontifex Maximus* of ancient Rome, and a national leader who could calmly stand in the dust of the Northern Territory in 1975 with equal aplomb, pouring sacred dirt into the hand of Gurindji traditional elder Vincent Lingiari, to symbolise the ceremonial return of traditional lands.

In reminding us of Whitlam's versatility and breadth, Pearson was offering Australia nothing less than a new way of conceiving national leadership: one that draws confidently upon the best of western culture *and* Aboriginal traditions.

And not coincidentally, Pearson burnished his own credentials as another such leader, capable of integrating our complex national history and various intellectual, spiritual and cultural legacies, and taking us hopefully towards a new and better national dispensation.

Seizing the moment

I read somewhere that the ailing Gough Whitlam planned his own funeral down to the last detail, and I suspect Noel Pearson had plenty of notice to prepare his magnificent speech.

But what happens when you are invited to give a major speech at little or no notice? How do you ensure that you are ready and able to do your best?

The Greeks, as always, had the word for it: *kairos*. It means timing: that exquisite and fleeting moment of opportunity familiar to every Australian who has ever tried and failed to bodysurf a passing wave. Get it right and you are a magnificent dolphin surging towards the shore. Get it wrong and you will be washed up bruised and grainy on the dank sand. Shakespeare said pretty much the same thing, if more eloquently, in *Julius Caesar*, when Brutus urges Cassius to grasp the opportune moment in their war against Mark Antony and Octavian (Act 4, Scene 3):

There is a tide in the affairs of men,
Which taken at the flood, leads on to fortune.
Omitted, all the voyage of their life
Is bound in shallows and in miseries.
On such a full sea are we now afloat.
And we must take the current when it serves,
Or lose our ventures.

Aristotle argued that *kairos* was a vital concept in speechmaking. An idea – or even a phrase – put forward at the wrong time can be disastrous, or at least fall flat. (If we think back to David Cameron's Bloomberg speech in Chapter 4, for example, one day we may conclude that this falls into the category of the right speech delivered at the wrong time.)

History is full of radical change that seemed impossible right up until the moment when it became inevitable – and we often associate those great moments with a great speech. When you buy a book of famous speeches, the first thing you'll look at is the name of the speaker: 'There they are,' you say, 'Churchill, or Lincoln, or Kennedy, or Elizabeth I.' But the second thing you look at is the date of their speech. That's because the most important speeches emerge under the pressure of historical turning points.

If you have a great story, you need to understand the right moment to tell it. The challenge – easy to recommend but hard to do – is to recognise that propitious tide as it rolls into view, and ride that wave.

Case study

Standing ready for your moment:
Prime Minister Julia Gillard in 2012

One of the most exhilarating examples of *kairos* in action in modern Australia occurred in 2012, when Prime Minister Julia Gillard rose to her feet in the Australian Parliament and gave opposition leader Tony Abbott a thorough dressing-down for his misogyny. Now, there had been many prior occasions on which the Prime Minister could have justifiably called out Tony Abbott's sexism in general and sexist attacks on her in particular. She deliberately, I suspect, chose not to respond on those earlier occasions, because to do so would have been to reveal too much of her rage and hurt. As Australia's first woman prime minister, she was perhaps unwilling to declare the offence she had taken, because it would have given her opponents the political gift of her wounded heart.

But this time was different, and the opportunity arose because Abbott had himself constructed it: he moved a motion that the Speaker of the House, Peter Slipper, be removed because of the allegedly sexist text messages he had sent to one of his aides. Given Tony Abbott's track record of public sexism, this was brazen hypocrisy, especially when he called the government's support for the Speaker 'another day of shame for a government which should already have died of shame'.

Later describing the moment as a 'crack point', the Prime Minister grasped the opportunity with unerring judgement. She used Abbott's hypocrisy rather than his misogyny as the pretext and pivot of her speech, urging him, if he wanted to know what misogyny looked like in modern Australia, to 'look in the mirror'.

But here's the point: the success of the speech did not lie in her righteous rage, exhilarating though it undoubtedly was, or its powerful tale of Abbott's misogyny. Its power lay in her readiness to deliver it, which, as Shakespeare told us, is all. She was able to seize the moment fully because she was prepared for it. With her lawyer's forensic clarity she stood up in the parliament and detailed example after example of Abbott's misogyny over many years, complete with dates and quotes and pithy suggestions that he might like to remind himself of his own track record by looking them up.

The now-famous Gillard misogyny speech appeared to be a spontaneous response to a particular moment, and in some senses it was. But it was a vintage performance that had surely been ripened through long cellaring. The greatest speeches can seem to emerge out of nowhere, right on cue, but if you look closely at their backstories, you will find that they are often the product of deep preparation, brooding, envisioning and sleepless rehearsal. And just waiting. That's how they emerge fully formed to seize the historic moment.

Using the run sheet to advantage

The concept of *kairos* or timing in the delivery of a speech usually relates to fleeting but historically significant opportunities. But we can also use more prosaic considerations of timeliness to advantage, including factors as simple as the mix, number and timing of other speeches on the day of delivery. Understanding the run-sheet ensures a speaker makes the most of their opportunity.

For example, President Lincoln was *not* the keynote speaker on that famous day in 1863 when he delivered the Gettysburg Address. That honour went to a well-loved public figure of the time, former secretary of state Edward Everett. Everett's speech lasted two hours and fulfilled many of the requirements of the ceremonial address. He spoke in detail about the course of the Battle of Gettysburg, and traced its significance all the way back to Pericles's 431 BCE funeral oration.

That left Lincoln, in many ways, rhetorically liberated. There were all kinds of ceremonial tasks he did not need to perform, because Everett had already done so. Lincoln was able to use his secondary spot to make his speech brief, with a narrower focus, and to his political advantage.

A great deal of modern public speaking occurs at conferences, where the speaker will be one of many. They may give a set-piece address on an advertised topic. Or deliver a short preliminary speech followed by a moderated panel discussion. There will be a speaker before and a speaker afterwards, or there will be lunch, dinner or drinks. The speechwriter will want to think about how the speaker must respond to, or benefit from, this particular set of circumstances. Ask the questions:

· What jobs will already have been done by other speakers?
· What points or arguments will already have been covered or raised?

- And then ... what is the job that only this particular
  speaker can do?

There are audience considerations, too. No one likes to speak straight after lunch, when audience energy levels are low. The end of the day is also hard work. But if allocated one of those slots, what can the speaker do to liven up the audience? It could be a simple matter of shortening the speech by five minutes, thereby creating more time for questions. Or opening the talk with some sparky rhetorical questions to challenge a dozy audience – and leaving them in some suspense about the answer until later in the presentation. Or maybe framing the speech as a dramatic case study, using one sustained example to exemplify your key points.

Often a senior leader will be asked to give a standalone set-piece speech at a lunch or dinner. Usually, someone will introduce them. The speaker might not only gracefully acknowledge the person introducing them, but refer to them as an example or inspiration or model of the key theme that they will be introducing in the speech.

When Geoff Dixon was CEO of Qantas, the media was well aware that he did not deliver set-piece speeches to accompany the announcement of his full-year or half-year results. Rather, the Qantas media team issued a succinct press release alongside the mandatory stock-exchange notice, and an hour later Geoff Dixon and his chief financial officer would walk into the press conference and say, 'Any questions?'

When he succeeded Dixon as CEO of Qantas, Alan Joyce communicated in a different way. Short set-piece speeches were delivered at the press conferences, before taking any questions. Any independent observer would have noticed that Joyce used these speeches not just to report on the recent past, but also to sell Qantas's strategic priorities and plans for the future. It might be argued that expecting bored, impatient journalists to wait through a 15-minute address before they could ask their questions was just begging for a backlash. But these days, journalists are under tremendous time pressure, and the speeches provided them with a framework of words and ideas they could use as a starting point for their questions and reports, which they did. When leaders are seen to step forward and explain their decisions in person and fully, they also enhance perceptions of their preparedness, confidence, openness and leadership.

Another key event for any public company is the annual general meeting. It is largely the chair's day, but an effective chair and CEO team will ensure that one gives a speech that looks back, while the other projects forward. The two speeches will then combine to offer a clear trajectory from the past to the present and ultimately the future. This will reinforce the strategic narrative, and help keep jaundiced shareholder eyes off any disappointments in the results, and on the positive opportunities that lie ahead. Look at the run sheet. Think about it. And use it to your advantage.

A better sorry

I conclude this chapter with consideration of two new persuasive challenges. This first is managing the apology for a personal or institutional failure. 'Sorry' used to be the hardest word, so a public apology was a rare thing. It was a grave matter for the speaker and heard by their audience with solemn respect. Remorse has traditionally been regarded as a socially valuable emotion in western culture; in common law the evidence of genuine contrition can even lessen the sentence for a crime.

Now people are forced to say sorry so often that 'sorry' has lost its value. Too often an apology is a convenient way to pre-empt public criticism or shut down a social media storm, and the novelty of a celebrity, sports person, business leader or politician flagellating themselves in public has well and truly worn off. Apologies have become as contagious as the flu. If it were a currency, the apology would be on a serious downward slide right now.

While watching the nightly TV news on just one evening, 31 May 2018, here's what I saw:

1. A Kiev journalist apologise for faking his own murder to thwart a possible Moscow plot.

2. Federal Health Minister Greg Hunt apologise for an outpouring of expletive-laden abuse directed at a 71-year-old grandmother.

3. The Anglican Church of Australia, Scouts Australia and the YMCA repeat their apologies to victims of child sexual abuse and announce that they were joining the $3.8 billion national redress scheme for survivors.

4. The Victorian Police apologise for as many as 25,000 phony random breath tests.

5. Southwest Airlines apologise because a staff member asked a passenger to 'prove' that her mixed-race son was related to her, despite providing his passport.

6. Various *Roseanne* employees apologise over Roseanne Barr's racist tweet, which had led the American Broadcasting Company to abruptly cancel the hit TV show after two months (while President Trump asked via tweet why *he* had not been apologised to for the mean statements made about *him* on that network).

7. White House press secretary Sarah Sanders tell a little boy that she was sorry to hear him say that he goes to school each day in fear of being shot.

That was just one night's TV viewing.

In Australia the banking royal commission has exposed so much immoral and potentially illegal behaviour that there has been a recent run of uncomfortable-looking banking and finance leaders appearing in public to express their regret for what their organisations or partners have done. With some variations, even the better of these apologies tend to adhere to a simple and fairly inadequate template:

- We apologise [insert preferred adverb: wholeheartedly, unreservedly, profoundly, without qualification] for our actions.

- We recognise that we have [insert preferred term of self-criticism: made mistakes, let you down, failed to meet community standards].

- We will do everything we can to [insert preferred objective: win back community confidence, earn back trust, restore our reputation].

- We are responding by [insert preferred course of action: undertaking a review, implementing new procedures, tightening standards, working to offer remediation to affected customers].

These tepid statements tend to be received, it seems to me, in a mood of weary public scepticism. They won't backfire exactly, but most people will fold their arms and wait without confidence to see whether the contrition leads to action.

It shouldn't be all that hard to say sorry in a way that is wholly truthful and therefore serves to restore some measure of trust. But the reality is that most public apologies don't do half the job they set out to do.

I think the first barrier to a good apology is a psychological one: pride. Chairs and CEOs are a particular breed: still mostly men, who are accustomed to lifelong achievement, praise and respect. In the natural order of things *other people* say sorry to *them*, so it must feel strange and wrong to be the one suddenly expected to do the apologising. Perhaps that's why we often hear a resistance creep into the language through the use of qualifiers. We are sorry *if* we let you down. We apologise to anyone who *may have felt* offended. The reluctance to own up is obvious.

The second barrier is in-house lawyers. They will try very hard to prevent any language that might be used against the corporation in court. So they will cross out an admission of 'wrongdoing' to replace it with 'missteps'. They will remove language about 'mistreating our customers' and replace it with 'letting people down'. This euphemistic language fools no one. It may protect the institution from litigation, but it will make the apology insincere and incomplete.

The third barrier is disconnection. 'This is not who we are,' says a CEO reassuringly to customers, 'and this is not what we stand for.' Quite evidently, however, it is exactly who they are and precisely what they stand for. Sometimes in the spirit of self-protection a senior head or two must roll to save the rest. Even so, the official language says that those departing bear no responsibility for any actual wrongdoing: 'We thank [the board member/CEO/senior executive] for their outstanding unblemished service over many years and we accept their resignation because we recognise that it's important that people are held to account.' Though this may have something to do with legal advice regarding the danger of appearing to admit guilt, the whole thing comes across as a cynical exercise in self-protection, driven by people who have become disconnected from ethics and reality.

The fourth barrier to a good apology is undue haste. Sometimes the rush to say sorry is a panicked capitulation to perceived or real public pressure. At other times a leader's overconfidence may lead to an assumption that a few reassuring words can make the problem go away. In March 2018, Australian cricket captain Steve Smith reportedly insisted on appearing at a press conference immediately after a match alongside junior player Cameron Bancroft to apologise for illegal ball-tampering, apparently believing that a token apology from him would be sufficient to resolve the issue quickly. But as Jane Cadzow wrote in the *Sydney Morning Herald* in June 2018, 'Smith's decision to come clean hadn't been triggered by a crisis of conscience. He and Bancroft had owned up to the plot ... for the simple reason that they had been sprung.' At the press conference Smith's tone was far too casual; he confused everyone's understanding of what had actually happened; and ultimately he made things far, far worse. If he had waited 24 hours before publicly responding, he might have begun to absorb and understand the rage and distress felt by the Australian cricket-loving public when it discovered that its heroes were cheats. This might have changed the timbre of his remarks for the better.

In the heat of a crisis, it is sometimes wiser not to rush out to smother the bad publicity. Better to quickly issue a brief initial holding statement: acknowledge that something has gone wrong; express concern that this has happened; confirm that all efforts are being made to rectify the problem in the short term; and promise that more will be said and done once the issues have been clarified. This provides some breathing space to focus clearly on what needs to be done and said next.

So how should a good apology work? Well, the psychologists recommend that to say a good sorry we should express genuine remorse, clearly acknowledge the feelings of those who have been injured, offer recompense, and provide assurance that there will be no repeat. Let me offer just a couple of refinements on that advice:

1. Be specific about the offence. The banking royal commission, for example, uncovered practices such as the extracting of fees from dead people, charging people for financial advice they didn't receive, giving people wrong or incomplete financial advice, forging loan documents and more. But it's remarkable how few finance leaders could actually bring themselves to name the misdemeanour for which they were apologising, instead confining themselves to a generic statement of regret. Say the facts, even if it hurts. At least it delimits the misdemeanour. A broad generic apology just leaves the impression that there may be more, as yet undeclared, offences.

2. Be specific about the victims. Who are they? Where are they? Can you name them (with their permission)? It might make sense to acknowledge those who have been

indirectly affected as well – the employees who go to work every day under a cloud, or even the Australian community, whose confidence has been shaken.

3. Clarify your relationship to the wrongdoing. Often when a chair or CEO stands up to say sorry, it sounds as though they have only the vaguest connection to the wrong that they are actually apologising for. You'd think they were distant observers, rather than actors in the events. Something bad happened and so, *noblesse oblige*, we had better just get on and apologise for it. It seems to me essential that the speaker should specify their own relationship to the wrong that was committed. Admittedly, sometimes a simultaneous external legal process or internal review is underway that complicates this, but I have no doubt that suitable words could be found: 'As chair, I am responsible, with the board, for governance of our company, and in this case there was a clear failure of governance.' Or: 'As CEO I should have done more to ensure there were sufficient resources devoted to the oversight of our external providers.' In the absence of this kind of specific testimony, the leader's apology appears tokenistic.

4. Describe as clearly as possible the proposed short-term and long-term response measures, plus explicit deadlines for getting them done.

5. Finally, read over your draft apology – which, if it includes points 1 to 4 above, will say what went wrong, who was affected and why you personally take some responsibility, and commits your organisation to taking action to compensate victims and ensure it doesn't happen again. Observe what you are thinking and how you are feeling while reading this draft, and imagine yourself saying the words aloud to an audience. If you still don't feel genuinely sorry then you probably should not apologise at all. People can tell when you're faking it.

Case study

A sorry that worked: Prime Minister Kevin Rudd in 2008

The most effective apology in Australian history was Prime Minister Kevin Rudd's apology to the Stolen Generations in 2008. Unlike most corporate apologies, which are forced out in a crisis situation, this speech had the benefit of long gestation and close consultation with the victims. It had been crafted to perfection. It's useful to look at the first few paragraphs of the speech, because they fully exemplify the points I made above:

> *I move that today we honour the Indigenous peoples of this land, the oldest continuing cultures in human history.*
> *We reflect on their past mistreatment. We reflect in particular on the mistreatment of those who were Stolen*

Generations – this blemished chapter in our nation's history.

The time has now come for the nation to turn a new page in Australia's history by righting the wrongs of the past and so moving forward with confidence to the future.

We apologise for the laws and policies of successive Parliaments and governments that have inflicted profound grief, suffering and loss on these our fellow Australians.

We apologise especially for the removal of Aboriginal and Torres Strait Islander children from their families, their communities and their country.

For the pain, suffering and hurt of these Stolen Generations, their descendants and for their families left behind, we say sorry.

To the mothers and the fathers, the brothers and the sisters, for the breaking up of families and communities, we say sorry.

And for the indignity and degradation thus inflicted on a proud people and a proud culture, we say sorry.

The speech was a job well done, and met with sighs of grateful relief around Australia. Note how specific the language is. The Prime Minister names the victims, identifies the wrongs committed against them, and refers to the impact of the wrongdoing. The repeated 'we say sorry' builds a rhythm. The full speech is a long one, and it incorporates extensive storytelling and the personal testimonies of individuals. It feels full and mature and satisfying, and lends hope.

Too often leaders regard an apology as a necessary evil, and approach it as an exercise to shut down the unpleasant conversation as fast as possible. That's the cynical view and it won't work. But, undertaken thoughtfully and in a spirit of integrity, a public sorry can be the product of careful self-assessment, and a great force for change and growth. It can even lay the foundations for a future of heightened trust.

The special case of the scientist

Finally we come to the special case of the scientist who wants to convince the world to act on his or her expert advice. It is one thing to note that 'elites' are no longer greatly trusted, but it is genuinely distressing to see that expert scientific or medical opinion is increasingly treated with careless dismissal. The continued success of the anti-vaccination activists or climate-change deniers is shameful testament to the trend.

In May 2018 the New South Wales Government announced that it would legislate to ban the culling of brumbies in the Kosciuszko National Park in recognition of the heritage value of the wild horses. The decision was made a few weeks after an independent expert committee found that these feral horses in Australia's alpine region were having a devastating impact on the brittle environment, degrading the soils and endangering numerous plant and animal species. David Watson, Professor of Ecology at Charles Sturt University, resigned from the New South Wales Threatened Species Scientific Committee in protest at the government's decision.

Is it any wonder the scientists and conservationists lost this particular battle? The only weapons they had to hand were some cold, hard environmental facts and a fragile, austere mountain ecology. Meanwhile, the campaign to save the brumbies was rich with emotive material: the legend of the young underdog 'stripling' on his 'small and weedy beast' from the Banjo Paterson poem *The Man from Snowy River*; the legacy of the bush pioneers; the romantic, visual appeal of the horses themselves.

It might be tempting to assume, then, that someone in my position would recommend that scientists adopt more of the tools of persuasion that I have been describing in this book, that I would encourage them to read my words and adopt the communication strategies that I have described. But I take a far more cautious view.

Certainly some scientists are natural communicators and can readily bring great storytelling and persuasion to the communication of their findings. I'm thinking of Carlo Rovelli on physics, or Iain McGilchrist (whose work I'll be mentioning later) on the brain.

And I'm encouraged by the passion of the young science students who take part in my communications courses. This emerging generation is keenly aware that science must not only be true but also widely accepted if it is to have the most productive impact. In a course on contemporary rhetoric, some of my science students created a campaign that included social media elements, great visuals and clear language to promote the benefits of vaccination.

But my overriding sense is this: scientists are a special case. They should never be tempted to compromise their academic integrity even for the worthy goal of promoting good science, because that risks derailing the scientific enterprise altogether.

Rather, we need stronger back-up for science by journalists, politicians, writers, artists, business leaders and all the other influencers who can carry scientific findings persuasively to a sceptical public. Alliances must be formed. It was, after all, the politician Al Gore's film *An Inconvenient Truth* (2006) that first moved the issue of climate change from the realm of science into popular consciousness. Beloved broadcaster David Attenborough has probably been more effective than anyone in raising environmental awareness, recently focusing attention on the curse of plastic in our oceans.

Ultimately it's far more important to the planet that scientists remain credible than that they become popular. So the rest of us must get better at heeding their advice and helping them to spread the message.

6

Crafting words that connect

WHEN I'M WRITING a major speech, I'm always in a state of nervous tension. It's physical. I am plonked in front of a screen and over a keyboard, but I'm not still. I'm either fidgeting or slouching; I'm rubbing my forehead or my thumbs. Before me looms that virtual white page, empty but for the speech title, the date and the name of the speaker. It doesn't matter that I know what the main and final message of the speech will be. It is irrelevant that I have a rough structure in mind.

I have gone to bed the night before knowing that this day is coming: this day when I'll finally have to knuckle down to *the draft*. I haven't slept at all well: a bare half-sleep, full of lurid dreams and visions. Sometimes on those restless nights, I will see words and paragraphs on my forehead. Once or twice, I have even heard them – quite loudly – in my inner ear: *Yes, that's it!* But the words stream past like uncaught fish in a fast-moving river.

By the time I get up in the morning, all the nervous tension has built to a pitch. I am desperate to begin, to make progress. Most of all, I'm hungry. I'm like some cranking 19th-century machine requiring vast amounts of energy. I'm my own stoker, and I start the day by shovelling muesli, yoghurt and coffee into the furnace. Then maybe another coffee. Then toast, perhaps with jam. Slowly, painfully, in the boiler room of the brain, things are heating up. My head feels warm. My earlobes get hot. My heart beats harder.

It's only when I'm totally fired up, with enough sustaining energy in me, that I can finally create what I have been looking for, and the heat-fuelled words materialise at last on the screen.

All that effort may only produce a few paragraphs, but these will be the critical introductory and framing concepts of the speech. They will provide the vantage point that sets up the whole network of themes that I propose to address. They will shape the way the audience hears and receives the arguments. They will carry the speech with a shining and inexorable logic through to its conclusion.

I'm so happy and relieved to have 400 good words on the page that I break for lunch. And, almost certainly, a nap. (Sleep is highly underrated as a creative tool. When you read political memoirs, there is often boasting about 'pulling all-nighters', but sleeplessness is often a source of mistakes and sloppiness. It's better to manage the body so that it is rested, if you can. Of course, often you can't.)

I am not alone in experiencing extreme speechwriterly anxiety. In his study of US presidential speechwriters, *White House Ghosts* (2008), Robert Schlesinger depicts all kinds of unhealthy behaviours that were no doubt brought on by the immense pressure of the job. The list of addictions ranges from cigarettes to caffeine to alcohol and even, in the case of Richard Nixon's speechwriters, amphetamines. One of George W Bush's speechwriters, Michael Gerson, wandered the West Wing corridors sucking so hard on the ends of pens that they routinely exploded in his mouth; it was described as a 'box-a-week' habit.

Here in Australia, Graham Freudenberg, the great Labor speechwriter, fuelled his writing with Dunhill cigarettes and loud recordings of Beethoven, surrounding himself for inspiration with busts of Lincoln, Churchill and Shakespeare.

Perhaps that explains why, along with the actual writing, there's a lot of coffee involved in drafting a speech. And walking around the block. And those short naps to reboot the brain.

Pros and cons of the 'shitty first draft'

One of the great bibles for writers, particularly fiction writers, is Anne Lamott's *Bird by Bird* (1995). It's a wonderful meditation on the craft and process of writing. One of her oft-quoted mantras is to push yourself to finish a 'shitty first draft'. It's an injunction that militates against the constipated perfectionism suffered by so many writers, and which often prevents them from making real progress.

I absolutely believe in the virtue of writing a shitty first draft of any piece of creative writing. It really means plodding along until you have a draft that you can mould and shape and work with. And when you are writing creatively, having created that shitty first draft, the next step might be to show a trusted reader, or put the thing aside before reading it again yourself in a while in order to grasp the possible next steps in the process.

But there are certain problems that arise in following this path with a speech. Deadlines, for one. Personnel, for another. Because the people who are likely to read your first drafts aren't writers, and aren't familiar with the exploratory and iterative nature of the writing process. They are pressed for time. They don't understand the adventurous probing of a first draft. They don't know how to read with a sense of the larger possibility of a speech. Instead, they operate out of a far more primitive paradigm. They are terrified of mistakes, for which they might get the blame. Often they waste their time scouring for what are, in their judgement, grammatical errors and typos, and spend their time inserting unnecessary commas or triumphantly putting apostrophes in the wrong place. They pounce on phrases that they think might offend, and ignore far larger philosophical or policy ideas that need to be clarified. Pettiness and pointlessness rule. Speechwriters are most likely to go completely mad when the wrong people read their first draft.

I have learned to get around this issue by explaining to potential readers of a draft speech the exact nature of their job. I might ask them to read purely for structure, or for facts, or for some other specific aspect. This is a way to stop pedants from 'improving' your prose.

When you circulate your first draft there is always that risk that enthusiastic would-be editors will meddle in your speech. But there's another risk too. Because once you have proved your worth as a speechwriter, and once the team thinks you are really good at your job, they may not want to touch your speech at all. If it looks even broadly okay, then everyone breathes a sigh of relief and moves on: 'Oh good, the speech is looking fine.' Everyone except you, because you know it's still just a first draft. So I've sometimes had to break every rule of corporate self-promotion by going around and undermining my own draft. I've been known to say to people, 'Well I think I may have exaggerated this,' or 'Are you sure we can really claim that?' At which point, people sigh and roll their eyes about the high-maintenance speechwriter and take another look.

The best editor I ever had was Syd Hickman, my former boss. When he wasn't hunting me down at Aussie's Café in Parliament House and ordering me to get back to the office and do some real work, he was talking me through a speech, carefully reading my drafts, and helping the speech fulfil its potential. He was so good at this that I had to marry him.

Obviously, that is not an option available to all speechwriters, so all I can counsel is that you find a reader – find *your* reader – someone who preferably is neither the speech-giver nor someone else with a direct stake in that particular speech. I have been lucky enough in most workplaces to find a sympathetic colleague who takes an interest in language and strategy; is prepared to read my drafts and give me an unvarnished opinion; and is kind (and confident) enough to warn me when I am not doing my best.

In this chapter we look at speechwriting in detail: voice, language, sentences, words, revisions and editing. The aim is to take you from the first draft to the best possible final version.

Find the voice of leadership: the voice that's better than yours

When we writers talk about voice, we are not wondering whether the character we are creating has a Cockney accent or a French one. We are not even talking about whether he or she is educated, or talks in jargon, or has a high-pitched tone. Voice is a deeper thing, one that is quite hard to define (hence the many different definitions in writing guides). Fiction writers predictably spend a lot of time thinking about voice, but perhaps more surprisingly, so do non-fiction writers. That's because even when you are ostensibly writing in your own voice, you have to make some major decisions about how that voice sounds.

I've published two non-fiction books – both personal essays written in the first person – and each had a different voice. My book on Paris, *True Pleasures*, had a tentative, almost wistful voice:

> As I hurry along the colonnades I can feel the soft
> weight of the scarf in its elegant shopping bag, and I
> already foresee its double future. In one version, I too

*possess that easy French elegance. I take the scarf out
of the drawer and drape it across my shoulders. Even
in my regulation black suit, I am lifted, lightened and
irradiated. In the other future, I fling and heave, I crush
and crinkle, and what looks so silken and sinuous when
tied upon me by a Parisienne merely looks lumpen when
adjusted by me …*

My book on manners, *Why Manners Matter,* was more
confident, stylised and teacherly:

*Manners are some of the limitations society imposes
to prevent one person's rights from infringing upon
another's. Sovereignty requires self-sovereignty. Or,
as Sigmund Freud put it more psychologically in
1930: 'It is impossible to ignore the extent to which
civilisation is built upon renunciation, the degree to
which the existence of civilisation presupposes that non-
gratification (suppression, repression or something else?)
of powerful instinctual energies.' Ah, repression. So sadly
undervalued in modern life.*

Even though the voices in those two books were very different,
they were still authentically my own, with my voice tempered
and shaped to meet the needs of each work.

Speechwriters also need to think about voice. I write for
leaders primarily, and it doesn't matter to me whether they

221

are old or young, highly educated or autodidacts. I am not employed because my clients want me to impersonate them on the page. After all, they know exactly how to sound like themselves. No. In a set-piece speech, they want to sound rather *better* than their everyday selves. They want to find out how it feels when the higher words unfurl off their tongue, how it feels to speak the language of leadership. Another way of saying this is that they want to sound like their very best selves, or better. That is, after all, the profound beauty and utility of the set-piece speech; it is one of the rare occasions when the words can be planned, refined and delivered as intended.

And so the voice I try to find for every leader is the voice of reason – or perhaps I should say the voice of *their* reason. Sane. Thoughtful. Knowledgeable. Trustworthy. These characteristics can be exhibited – or undermined – in every aspect of the speech, from the structure, to the formulation of each sentence, to the quality of the argument.

This may sound like I'm making a case for dull, bland and uniform speeches – stale, old, *reasonable* ones – but I'm not. The voice of reason in speeches is a rare and marvellous thing. There's nothing like the relief you feel as a citizen when someone gets up and plainly outlines a commonsense and honestly held point of view that you feel persuaded by in your very bones.

When I first set to work on a speech, in my mind I imagine I'm writing for someone rather like but a little bit better than my client, and certainly better than me. My overriding objective is to write in a way that's true and logical and easy to follow.

I write speeches for people who have things of import to say, and need to present their arguments in a cogent, clear and persuasive manner.

Case study

Talk like a prime minister: Prime Minister Bob Hawke

When I had the opportunity to write my first professional speech – a minor ceremonial speech for Prime Minister Hawke – I set eagerly about the task. At first, I assumed that my experience in writing the talking points for the Prime Minister's private meetings (as discussed earlier in the book) would help me. But speechwriting is different; it requires a larger imaginative leap.

The speech was a short welcome address, to be given at a lunch for a South Pacific leader. I spent a long time trying to imagine I was the Prime Minister. *What does Bob Hawke want to say?* I'd ask myself. *What does Bob Hawke want to say about the South Pacific?* I'd wonder. *What does Bob Hawke want to say to this South Pacific leader?*

Of course, it was all too big for me. How on earth could a 27-year-old woman imagine herself in the shoes of this trade-union legend, political titan and world figure? This one-time drinking and womanising, larger-than-life bloke? I went through the first of many restless, lurid pre-drafting nights.

It was more out of a sense of desperation than anything else that I came upon an alternative approach. It involved an act of *hubris*. Instead of trying to imagine myself in Bob Hawke's shoes, I decided to imagine myself in his *job*. I didn't ask, *What would Bob Hawke want to say?* I chose to ask myself, instead, *If I were prime minister, what would I want to say?*

Almost immediately, the task became clearer to me. As I imagined myself prime minister, standing in that Great Hall of Parliament House, smiling graciously at my guest seated next to me and looking out over the large, expectant assembly, I realised that the speech could be as simple and inevitable and truthful as this:

Welcome, we're so glad to have you here. Your friendship is important to us. For many years we have worked together on causes great and small. Here are some of the good things we have achieved together. Here are some of the great things you've done yourself. Now we are meeting to discuss important matters, some easy, others more complex. We do so in a spirit of good will, building upon all that we have achieved together in the past, and with great hopes for the future.

I can't remember how that particular speech turned out. But I do know that insight was the beginning of my career as a speechwriter. Having catapulted myself imaginatively into the role of prime minister, from then on I had no hesitation in presuming to run a bank, an airline, a ministry, a statutory authority. By placing myself not in Bob Hawke's shoes, but in his job, I was able to haul myself up to the level required to think like a leader. Like *the* leader.

Since that moment, it has been important for me as a speechwriter to go within myself, to imaginatively place myself in the speaker's role and draw on my own human values. Speechwriting is not a transcription service, but a creation service. The words don't just reflect an idea; very often, they also shape and crystallise it.

Convolution, cliché, plagiarism and platitude

When I first went to work for Kim Beazley, I despaired of ever being able to collaborate successfully with him. His sentences were extraordinarily convoluted, though perfectly, even infuriatingly, grammatical. His favourite ploy was to defer; it might be five clauses before he arrived at the point of a sentence. Syd Hickman had a theory that this was one of Beazley's astute political defence tactics: deferring the definitive statement until you were quite sure you had qualified your way around any potential trouble. Even though the grammar and reasoning were entirely sound, they just didn't *sound* sound.

So in this case, I saw my job as being – in large measure – about making Beazley's sentences a little easier to digest, so that they sounded as reasonable as the terrific ideas behind them. My strategy was to turn his sentences on their end: I'd start with the main final point then I'd turn the five clauses, if they were still required, into short explanatory sentences. He would be able to recognise his logic, if not his natural style. And the audience would hear a lucid, reasonable, easy-to-follow line of thought.

It was easy enough in Beazley's case to find his voice of reason buried within his language, because he was a very smart and sane individual. But sometimes the problem goes deeper than mere sentence structure. Sometimes the leader's thoughts appear to be dull or commonplace or even clichéd. When I was a novice speechwriter, I would try to ameliorate these drawbacks by inserting quotations from famous thinkers into leaders' speeches. Everyone from management guru Peter Drucker to political philosopher Machiavelli got a run. I had some foolish idea that this was an important part of the value I could add to the speeches. My deep well of reading would make ordinary speeches sound better than they really were.

Big mistake. I now blush at the memory. Except in rare circumstances, leaders should have moved beyond the need to appeal to other authorities for a justification or explanation of their own thoughts. Leaders don't quote people, I've come to believe. People quote leaders.

Sometimes a passion for quoting can be taken to such embarrassing extremes it becomes plagiarism. I can't think of any English-language dramatist since Shakespeare who has loved speeches as much as Aaron Sorkin, or who has done more to popularise them in the modern era. And sometimes people love Aaron Sorkin's speeches so much they feel the need to borrow his words for themselves. In 2012, the Federal Minister for Transport, Anthony Albanese, gave an address to the prestigious National Press Club in Canberra in which he memorably drew upon the speech Michael Douglas delivered as a US president and romantic-comedy hero in Aaron Sorkin's

1995 film *The American President*. Michael Douglas's character had said:

We have serious problems to solve, and we need serious men to solve them. And whatever your particular problem is, I promise you, Bob Rumson is not the least bit interested in solving it. He is interested in two things and two things only: making you afraid of it and telling you who's to blame for it.

Albanese's version went like this:

In Australia, we have serious challenges to solve and we need serious people to solve them. Unfortunately, Tony Abbott [then Liberal leader of the opposition] is not the least bit interested in fixing anything. He is only interested in two things: making Australians afraid of it and telling them who's to blame for it.

I still love *The American President*, but let's face it, that was a terrible speech. It is both completely hilarious and utterly bewildering that an Australian federal minister once adopted it for his own. The joy of the movies – especially American movies – is that an entirely sentimental and egoistic speech can save a flagging presidency, win the girl, and make our hero a legend. In real life, it's not quite that easy.

Most leaders won't follow Albo's example and pinch a few words, but they may over-quote other people's ideas. In the late 1990s, in my very early days as a freelancing corporate speechwriter, I had a meeting with the CEO – also newish to his role – of a major Australian technology firm. We were preparing for a significant speech about the emerging impact of email and the internet. The atmosphere was rather awkward. The CEO seemed uncertain about where to begin, and I wasn't altogether sure how to help him.

His adviser prompted, 'We're just back from Switzerland. Why don't you download your out-takes from Davos [the high-powered annual economic forum]?'

At this point, the CEO began telling me all the things that *other* business leaders were thinking about the internet, how 'they thought' it was likely to expand around the world, and how 'they judged' the impact of email, and how 'they believed' this new online environment would profoundly challenge and disrupt conventional communications. I was rather thrown by this, but as I began working with different clients I discovered, to my surprise, how often it happens. Business leaders, like anyone else, can lack confidence. So they default, at least initially, to accepted business wisdom. They mouth the clichés of consultants or the platitudes of respected peers rather than risking their own opinions in public. Whether it's the future of productivity, or the state of the resources industry, or reforms in tertiary education, they'll relay to me the comments they've read in the *Financial Review* that morning, or remarks they heard other business people say about the topic at the last conference they went to. It's as if they want to impersonate being a leader rather than actually be one.

With the benefit of a lot more experience, I no longer fret about the standard of modern leadership (or at least, not so much). Nor do I interrupt this copycat process; I'll let them talk it out. Because gradually, as they hear themselves speak, as they talk themselves into the topic, sooner or later they will stop parroting the views of other people and their own genuine thinking will emerge. It might be 10 or 15 minutes into their remarks when a signal alerts me. A surprise digression. A quickening of the voice. A sudden, thoughtful hesitancy. *That's it*, I'll think. That's where the authentic, original thinking is to be found.

I'll start to engage, to push for more thoughts, to ask for more detail. With any luck, the conversation will gain momentum and the ideas will flow. I will discover the reasoning behind the ideas, and generally it's sound, and I suddenly understand why this particular leader got their job in the first place. My job will be to convert that authentic flow of ideas into a full persuasive argument.

A leader is not an analyst or an academic. And a leader's speech is neither a personal essay nor a lecture. So it should neither be overly introverted nor unduly contemplative. It definitely should not defer the main message until the conclusion. A leader's speech works best as the resolved product of thinking, not a record of the thinking process. The voice of reason always has an integrity and a sense of resolution.

Ways to lift and enliven your speech

Do you happen to recall the song 'I Will Always Love You'? It was written by Dolly Parton and memorably performed by Whitney Houston in the 1992 film *The Bodyguard*. I think it's quite likely you *can* remember it. Not necessarily because you love it. On the contrary, you may wince as the melody comes into your mind. But you haven't forgotten the song, perhaps because it has one of the all-time most unforgettable pop-music key changes, when it suddenly shifts its centre of gravity to a higher key. As Houston's magnificent, gospel-choir-trained voice charges upwards, she lifts the song from a sweet farewell salute to an aching lament for lost love. Whatever you may think of it, that song has *grip*.

Key changes are the most obvious and showy form of 'modulation', a term that encompasses various techniques to expand the emotional range of a piece of music. As every rock star knows, if a song is boring, a key change is often the solution. It heightens the intensity.

If we were to think of speeches as pieces of music, we might conclude that many speeches could do with some modulation too. They are so often flat and uniform from start to finish. The speaker takes a breath at the beginning and then drags on and on in exactly the same tone until the words run out.

Speeches, like music, are aural. Modulation in speeches can work the same way as key changes in music, to add vibrancy and emphasis. And, as in music, there are some fairly simple techniques that can be adopted to lift speeches to a higher or more intense level.

Tell 'em about the dream

Once I was writing a major strategy speech for a client whose business was in big trouble. My draft was very clear about the problems facing the company and the harsh but necessary solutions. I circulated the speech to a range of people for feedback. One of them pulled me up short, saying to me over the phone, 'Look, I think it's fine. You've explained why the business needs to change. You've described the dire consequences if it doesn't. You've also written about the solutions to the problem. But it's not enough. There's a step missing. I'm wondering: if we believe success can be achieved, then what will it actually look like?'

At that moment I was suddenly reminded of something. My writers' group sometimes organises informal seminars on aspects of the craft. One of the most interesting sessions was led by screenwriter and director David Roach, known for *Young Einstein, Beneath Hill 60* and *Red Obsession* among other films. David took us through his adapted version of the famous 'hero's journey' story structure, the renowned template for screenwriting in which the hero goes through a range of trials before achieving his quest. One point particularly resonated with me. David spoke about the technique of inserting a small scene at the darkest stage of the journey. The aim is to let the audience glimpse the better world that our hero is dreaming of. The ideal. The utopia. And this is valuable because it reminds the audience of the importance of the prize, and the worthiness of the quest.

Case study

Key change: Dr Martin Luther King Jr in 1963

In 1963, Dr Martin Luther King Jr gave his famous speech calling for an end to racism, at the Lincoln Memorial in Washington, DC. This speech too is a list of problems and potential solutions. Or could have been. 'We can never be satisfied,' thundered Dr King:

> *... as long as the Negro is the victim of the unspeakable horrors of police brutality. We can never be satisfied as long as our bodies, heavy with the fatigue of travel, cannot gain lodging in the motels of the highways and the hotels of the cities ... We can never be satisfied as long as our children are stripped of their self-hood and robbed of their dignity by signs stating: 'For Whites Only.' ... No, no, we are not satisfied, and we will not be satisfied until justice rolls down like waters, and righteousness like a mighty stream.*

Dr King could, with great justice, have concluded the speech with those stern judicial terms: justice and righteousness. But, according to the legend, just at that point in his address, the great gospel singer Mahalia Jackson – and I think it was no coincidence that a musician had this instinct – called out to her friend, 'Tell them about the dream, Martin!'

And it was at that point, it seemed, that Dr King began to ad-lib the most famous, potent and inspirational riff of the speech: 'I have a dream!' No less than seven times he called out, 'I have a dream!' as he painted his inspiring portrait of a future, equal America. Then he landed on his final vignette:

I have a dream that my four little children will one day live in a nation where they will not be judged by the color of their skin but by the content of their character. I have a dream!

'Little children'. Note the biblical simplicity of that phrase.

We know that speech now as the 'I have a dream' speech. That was the key change that took the speech to another level. And why we remember it as one of the greatest of all time. Tell 'em about the dream.

Repeat yourself

Like musicians, preachers know all about repetition. The call-and-response technique is a powerful way to connect speaker and audience, and each repeated phrase scales the sermon up to a higher intensity. The logical side of the brain takes a break, and the emotions take over.

Repetition can do many things: help people absorb and remember, create a catchphrase, give people time to get the joke, slow the speech down, give it weight and gravitas.

These aren't the only uses for repetition. Every young speechwriter I know despairs of translating the jargon used by senior management in their speeches and presentations. Often they feel too intimidated either to admit they haven't the faintest idea what the prospective speaker is talking about, or to try to convince them that no one who is actually human will understand it either.

One approach is not to fight the experts. Let them make their point in their ghastly jargony way, even in the speech. In a speech I worked on for then finance minister Kim Beazley, around the time of the privatisation of Qantas, we sought to explain the rationale behind the government's privatisation program. There were lots of technical economic arguments laid out in the speech for those who were interested. But we also wanted to speak to ordinary Australians who feared the demise of their iconic Australian airline if it went out of public hands. So in the speech we argued that in Australia less than 50 years earlier, federal and state governments had owned everything from brickworks to butchers' shops, fishing trawlers to fruit canneries. We then wrote something like, 'You wouldn't expect the government to own butchers' shops today, and in much the same way, it no longer makes sense to own an airline.'

The two versions of the explanation – the technical and the conversational – can go into the speech. In such cases, it is not the words that get repeated, but the concept, tailored to different audiences. This use of repetition means both the experts and the broader audience get the information in a way they can well understand. Journalists are particularly grateful for vivid, simple analogies. And the change of image alongside the repetition of meaning creates an energising shift in modulation.

Another way to create a change in mood and emphasis through repetition is to use the pointed digression. In this case, you might tell a story that apparently has only a tangential relationship to the matter at hand. This wakes everyone up and gets their attention. Then you can bring the point of the story back to your central thesis.

In President Clinton's speech at the Democratic National Convention in 2012, mentioned earlier, Clinton digresses to the experience of his own presidency in order to demonstrate a point about the merits of the Obama presidency. He used an argument by example to lend weight to his case that the benefits of the Obama Administration's economic policy might not yet, but would be sure to, flow. The digression was a way of repeating the argument in a different way.

Case study

Repetition as roadmap: President John F Kennedy in 1962

Great speeches tell the truth. But more and more we don't get honesty; rather, we get boastful words and over-promising. It's one reason for the loss of trust. Politicians in particular are guilty of announcing ambitious long-term projects as if they are already fully guaranteed, when in fact there are very many uncertainties, hurdles and obstacles to be faced along the way. With every setback the public becomes more cynical, and weak leaders are easily tempted to give up. How many times have we heard a business leader or politician declare a rock-solid commitment to something – a principle, a deadline, an accomplishment – then slither their way out of their promise at the first sign of trouble?

In 1962, President John F Kennedy (with the aid of his speechwriter and counsellor Ted Sorensen) spoke to an audience at Rice University in Texas about the future of space exploration, and delivered one of the boldest promises in human history:

We choose to go to the moon. We choose to go to the moon in this decade and do the other things, not because they are easy, but because they are hard, because that goal will serve to organize and measure the best of our energies and skills, because that challenge is one that we are willing to accept, one we are unwilling to postpone, and one which we intend to win, and the others, too.

'We choose to go to the moon.' So grand an idea, conveyed by so simple a sentence. Note the 'we', which implies a warm, human, collective enterprise. Note the verbs 'choose' and 'to go', which emphasise movement and action. If he were a typical leader today, JFK would probably be advised to say, 'The government is committed to a moon landing by April 1967.' It would be a statement deadened by bureaucratic language, cynically promising an unachievable completion date, and sneakily relying upon a subtle get-out clause. Because if it is the government that has committed itself to the project, then that same, or any future, government (for they are, after all, anonymous and interchangeable) can renege on the promise.

The leader making that promise removes him or herself from responsibility for its achievement.

Kennedy's speech was notably unlike most modern political speeches. It sought to inspire and excite people about the prospect of moon exploration. But it was also prepared to say honestly that a difficult path lay ahead. Kennedy continued:

> *To be sure, we are behind, and will be behind for some time in manned flight. But we do not intend to stay behind, and in this decade, we shall make up and move ahead ...*

And again:

> *To be sure, all this costs us all a good deal of money ... [If we are going to] do all this, and do it right, and do it first before this decade is out – then we must be bold.*

And then came a quite remarkable paragraph in which Kennedy said:

> *However, I think we're going to do it, and I think that we must pay what needs to be paid. I don't think we ought to waste any money, but I think we ought to do the job. And this will be done in the decade of the sixties. It may be done while some of you are still here at school at this college and university. It will be done during the term of office of some of the people who sit here on this platform. But it will be done. And it will be done before the end of this decade.*

If a leader spoke like this today – intermingling surging optimism with little backward retreats into doubt, hesitation and lack of commitment – we would think they were crazy. We would ask what the hell Kennedy really meant; did he actually think the United States could get to the moon within a decade or not?

But this was Kennedy planting into American minds the rhythm of the project through the rhythm of his words – how it would advance through a process of trial and error, setback and breakthrough, hopes raised and hopes temporarily dashed. Kennedy was helping his country understand that long-term success would require an adaptation to short-term failure, and that it would need patience, fortitude and inner self-belief if it were to succeed. The forward and backward rhythm of the speech foreshadowed the iterative process that was to come: an emotional journey of hope, doubt, grief and ultimate triumph.

Kennedy announced the moon mission in September 1962. He was assassinated in Texas in November 1963. And in July 1969, achieving Kennedy's promise, Neil Armstrong became the first human to walk on the moon.

Kennedy ended his speech with these words:

Many years ago the great British explorer George Mallory, who was to die on Mount Everest, was asked why did he want to climb it. He said, 'Because it is there.' Well, space is there, and we're going to climb it, and the moon and the planets are there, and new hopes for knowledge and peace are there. And, therefore, as we set sail we ask

God's blessing on the most hazardous and dangerous and greatest adventure on which man has ever embarked.

This speech is commonly described as inspirational, but its inspiration does not rely upon a forecast of, or exhortation to, inevitable success. Rather, its power lies in repeated expressions of faith in the face of doubt, and its trust that Americans will stay the course until they achieve their goal.

Zoom in, zoom out ...

In Chapter 4, I mentioned the power of thinking in terms of vantage points. I observed that the leader is in the fortunate position of having access to both the widest possible view and the smallest detail.

When a draft feels flat and monotonous, have a think about switching the perspective. Is it time to go up a level to the grand bigger picture? How about switching down to the small but telling detail? Zooming in or out can give a big energy boost to a flat speech.

Case study

Switch perspectives to energise a speech: Deputy Prime Minister Kim Beazley in 1995

In November 1995 I wrote a speech for Kim Beazley to deliver to the Annual Conference of the Federation of Ethnic Communities Council of Australia. He was delivering it in the capacity of acting prime minister – the Prime Minister was overseas – so it felt like a big deal. It was an opportunity to show his leadership potential to the powerful and influential ethnic lobby.

The first draft was about the power of Australia's diverse multicultural society, and the policy measures that the government was taking to ensure that we continued to build our nation for the 21st century. It was all very worthy and high-level. But it had no heart. So we had to find a way to bring that story to life, with more images, more delicacy, more feeling.

This was what Beazley said on the night:

Before I conclude tonight I want to point to two historical markers – one behind us, and one which lies ahead. This year we celebrate the 50th anniversary of the commencement of post-war migration to Australia – the year that really sparked the substantial shift to a multicultural Australia.

History again. It comes in very handy as a means not only to find the overall vantage point, but also to find new perspectives and angles within a speech. As I was drafting this new section of the speech, an image embedded deep in my memory surfaced. My early years were spent in Sydney's western suburbs. Our neighbours, the Schindlers, had fled ravaged Vienna after World War II and come to Australia with their two little boys. They had left behind them the grave of their beloved daughter, a little girl killed in the Allied bombing of Vienna in 1944. Whenever we visited them for some of Mrs Schindler's legendary sponge cake, my brother and I would gaze at that solemn little black-and-white face on the sideboard, and wonder who she was and what it all meant. So the next lines were written with the Schindlers in mind:

For many individuals I am sure that this anniversary brings back some complex memories of the war and the painful, life-changing decisions it required. Many thousands of people came to Australia with nothing more than a few belongings and a small black-and-white photo of a loved one.

Afterwards, many people came up to Beazley and asked him 'how he knew' about their photo. The power of the small, telling detail. Beazley went on to describe the impact of those waves of immigrants on Australia:

They made their home here, they gave this country their loyalty and their hard work. They raised a new generation of young Australians. For Australia this anniversary is unashamedly a cause for mighty celebration. The tolerant, cosmopolitan and open Australia we have today rides substantially on the wave of post-war immigration.

As we look to those days we remember that it was the search for democracy, freedom and opportunity which drew so many to Australia; we acknowledge the cultural riches brought to this country by waves of courageous

individuals; and we recognise the generosity of those
who welcomed so many settlers to our nation. Most of
all, we celebrate the great, tolerant, modern and diverse
society we have achieved together in a remarkably short
period of time.

And now there was another switch in historical perspective, but
this time to an imagined future:

Now let us fast forward momentarily and imagine the
world spotlight on Australia in 2000. It is four years after
the Atlanta Olympics in the United States and one year
before the centenary of our coming together in Federation.
I hope the Republic will be a reality for us by then.

Thousands of athletes will have come to Australia from
around the world, along with their families, international
dignitaries and millions of tourists. Watching the games
on televisions around the world will be a billion viewers in
Asia, in North America and Europe.

No doubt they will be struck by the physical beauty
and grandeur of this continent. They will be surprised
by a truly modern nation – at the leading edge of new
information and communication technologies, and at the
forefront of environmental technologies. They will sense
a sophisticated community, comfortable with its place in
the world, looking forward to the next century.

But what they will remember most is that a nation
of startling diversity is at the same time one of the

most cohesive, inclusive places on the planet. They will remember that for all the many cultures, we are truly one nation. As we look to the year 2000, that most resonant of years in modern times, there is no doubt in my mind that Australia can and should be the nation that most closely captures the spirit of the age.

Quite often, you won't recognise either the need or the opportunity to zoom in or out until you have drafted the substance of the speech. It's in the revision process that you can tell the flat points, usually when you find your eyelids gently closing as you peruse your own prose. That's when you know it's time to energise the text. Then it's a matter of ranging imaginatively over the material, rather like a camera lens searching for the most powerful image and scaling it to the right size.

Rent-a-head

The Preface to this book consists of a series of aphoristic remarks about the art and craft of the speech and the role of the speechwriter. I came up with this section one day when I was bored by my own style and wished I could write like someone who could write better than me. So in that instance, I briefly rented the head of the witty French writer François de la Rochefoucauld, channelled via Oscar Wilde's preface to *The Picture of Dorian Gray*.

'Rent-a-head' is a technique used in my writing group to open up new thought channels and give us access to different minds. We developed the idea from some remarks made by one of Australia's leading advertising executives, Todd Sampson. So, depending on our tastes and subject, we might rent Saul Bellow for the day, or Jane Austen, or Helen Garner.

I wrote my book *True Pleasures* while frequently renting the head of Nancy Mitford, and *Why Manners Matter* occasionally channelling essayists Clive Bell and Harold Nicolson. It was fun to write like this. It gave me a break from my own style – or perhaps it would be more accurate to say that it helped me find the shade of my own voice that was appropriate for each book. I used these writers and their work not so much to copy the way they wrote, but to embrace something of their spirit – the aristocrat lightness of Nicolson and the dash and dare of Nancy Mitford.

Sometimes it works, sometimes it doesn't. But whenever you feel fatigue at the limitations of your own style, you might want to try it. It's a fast way to give the piece more energy.

By the way, renting a head is not at all the same thing as quoting someone's words. Sure, you can drop a quote from Shakespeare or Churchill into a speech and it will certainly create some kind of change of mood. But in my experience – and perhaps it's because I am so often looking at my own pedestrian drafting – rather than lifting the piece, it only serves to emphasise the limitations of one's own style. This is another reason – on top of those I discussed earlier – why I am very dubious about the merits of quotes in my own speeches: who wants to see how much better someone else said it? So when I am talking about renting a head, it is not at all about using that head's exact words. It's deeper than that.

You might imagine I would recommend that any speechwriter or leader looking to rent a head should automatically turn for inspiration to the great leaders and their speeches. And many people have most definitely tried to rent the heads – and yes, the words – of Churchill and Shakespeare and Dr King. But I would not suggest turning to a great speech for inspiration unless you know the full backstory to it. There's not much point reading any speech in isolation. You need to know the circumstances surrounding it. You need to know a bit about the political and social context, the aims of the speech, the points of resistance in the audience, and the speech's immediate impact and longer-term effects. That's one of the many reasons why speechwriters tend to be avid readers of history – it helps them understand the circumstances in which key speeches were created and the role they have played in world events.

In any case, there are many other, often more effective, sources of inspiration. If I am mounting a difficult argument, I like to read the words of writers with wickedly independent minds like Voltaire, Edmund Burke, Theodore Dalrymple and Christopher Hitchens. Their writing reminds me that it's possible to hold and express politically incorrect views and get away with it. (Or at least most of the time. Voltaire was bashed, imprisoned and effectively exiled for some of his more exuberant writings against royal tyranny and the Church. I seem to recall Christopher Hitchens made many enemies through his views on Mother Teresa and the war in Iraq. These are perhaps useful reminders that writing – and speaking – can be dangerous and courageous acts.)

On other occasions, I might decide to adopt something of a teaching mode, and then I turn to tremendous communicators like Michael Lewis on finance and Wall Street, Howard Goodall on music, and Bill Bryson on just about anything. These are people who take dense technical information and make it extremely accessible and entertaining without losing any of its quality.

Then there's always George Orwell, the touchstone of plain and moral English at its best. And though the political positioning of *The Economist* magazine feels a bit out of date nowadays, the clarity and style of language remain marvellous. A shot of *The Economist* is always good for a speechwriter trying to escape from the fog of jargon.

Case study

The power of metaphor: psychiatrist Iain McGilchrist in 2009

In 2009, Dr Iain McGilchrist, psychiatrist, writer and literary scholar, wrote an important book, *The Master and His Emissary*, about the different but complementary roles played by the left and right hemispheres of the human brain.

When I was growing up the left brain was considered the side of the brain worth cultivating. It was logical, dominant, organised and reasonable. The right brain, by contrast, was considered messy, creative and emotional. If you wanted to be a leader when you grew up, you definitely wanted to be a left brain kind of person.

McGilchrist's work outlines the recent advances in neuroscience and debunks this way of thinking. He explains that the left brain is not the master after all; in fact it is just the emissary, a kind of 'high functioning bureaucrat' that is good at carrying out orders. The right side of the brain is the master side; the realm of perspective, meaning-making, far-sightedness, and context; the very attributes we need in modern leaders.

McGilchrist argues that in the modern world we have come to value the attributes of the left brain at the expense of the right brain. I see this in nearly every corporation I work with. Let's face it, in nearly every sphere of modern life bureaucracy has gone mad. Paperwork (or online form-filling) is never ending. Jargon has replaced clear and vivid speaking. And too often leaders sound rather like bureaucrats, as if they are diligently carrying out someone else's orders.

McGilchrist's ideas are compelling and persuasive. This is partly because of the brilliant way he expresses them, through the extensive use of metaphors. The very title of McGilchrist's book is a metaphor, of course, based upon a story by the philosopher Nietzsche.

To explain the brain's hemispheres to a non-expert like me he uses the simple analogy of a bird that uses high-beam *right-brain* attention to spot a danger in the environment (such as the approach of a bird of prey), and deploys narrow-beam *left-brain* attention to pick up a seed against a background of grit. Effective and easily remembered.

McGilchrist employs a different analogy to appeal to his scientific peers. He says in a radio interview: 'You could think of the left hemisphere's world as a bit like what Newtonian mechanics told us the world was like; fixed objects that hit one another and cause things and so on. But the right hemisphere's view is more like what we now know from quantum mechanics, that it is uncertain, unstable, constantly changing and flowing, but much, much richer, this reality, although it's harder to grasp.'

McGilchrist's work reminds us that metaphors aren't just an enjoyable rhetorical flourish. They provide a way for leaders to fully convey their thinking to the various members of their audience. People often regard speechwriting as a purely left-brain activity, a simple case of transcribing ideas into words onto a page, a bureaucratic exercise. But great leaders' speeches are led by the right brain, because the speeches are about the bigger picture and meaningful connections. When we use powerful metaphors in speeches we are activating the right brain, the leader's side of the brain.

Use the structure

People often misunderstand the nature of suspense in storytelling. They think suspense occurs when you don't know what's going to happen. Wrong. Suspense occurs when you are quite sure you know what's going to happen but don't know *how*.

Letting your audience know the structure of your speech is an extremely effective tool for creating suspense, and lending some nervous energy and anticipation to their reception of it. This is where the old adage comes in handy: 'Tell them what you're gonna tell 'em. Tell them. Then tell them what you told 'em.'

When you tell people at the outset what the structure is, at one level it makes them relax into your speech, because it signals that you have prepared your remarks and set parameters around them (audience interpretation: 'Thank God, this won't go on forever'). Even during the most wonderful speeches – and certainly those I have drafted myself – I mentally tick off the sections as they are delivered and calculate how long it will be until the speech ends. I always feel worried and sometimes furious if I think a speech is going over time.

A statement about structure should be bald and clear:

· 'I have three things to say.'
· 'This is my argument and today I will give you three reasons for it.'

But if you convey your structure with some care and sly attention to drama, you can also create interest and suspense:

· 'And thirdly, I will take up the controversial issue of ...'
· 'Finally, I'll explain how we are going to bring this ambitious program to completion in record time.

The other great reason for being open about structure is that at each well-signalled turning point in the speech, the speaker has an opportunity to change the tone. The opening of any new section, when the speaker says, 'Now let me turn to ...', might herald a turn towards a serious matter, a piece of good news, a big idea, or a subject of special interest to one particular group.

You can adopt this tone purely for one section of the speech, giving the speech range and variation.

Be alert to the uses of structure. A clear structure is an elegant and simple way to give dramatic tension to the speech.

Switch the pronoun

Listen to the pronouns that leaders choose to deploy. Some leaders like to refer to 'we', 'us' and 'our'. It's a way of emphasising that all that has been achieved is due to the team effort. It strikes a less hierarchical, more collegial note. On the downside, 'we' can sound a bit like sharing the blame around if things are going wrong. Other leaders prefer to use 'I' and 'my'. They will talk about 'my executive team' or 'my approach'. This has the virtue of emphasising that the leader takes personal responsibility, but can also risk sounding arrogant.

One way to create a key change in a speech is to switch the pronoun. If a leader uses the 'I' voice then switches to 'we' or 'you', it will have an immediate, dramatic effect. And 'you' can be electric, if used well.

Case study

Pronouns that tap into emotions:
Market Basket CEO Arthur T Demoulas in 2014

One speech using the switching-pronouns technique was given off the back of a truck in Connecticut in August 2014. CEO Arthur T Demoulas had been engaged in an almighty struggle for control of Market Basket, the discount supermarket business started by his father. Nearly 25,000 grocery workers had gone on strike when Arthur T was sacked as CEO by the company's family-run board. Customers joined in the Market Basket revolt and so did social media. The story became a sensation, broadcast across America. Just one month after the worker uprising began, the board caved in and agreed to sell the company to Arthur T and his side of the family.

Next morning, Arthur T drove to where the workers were gathered, got up on the back of a truck and gave a rallying, joyous speech. Note the interesting use of pronouns:

You have demonstrated that everyone here has a purpose. You have demonstrated that everyone has meaning and no one person is better or more important than another, and no one person holds a position of privilege. Whether it's a full-timer or a part-timer. Whether it's a sacker, or a cashier, or a grocery clerk, or a truck driver, or a warehouse selector, a store manager, a supervisor, a customer, a vendor or a CEO – we are all equal. By working together – and only together – do we succeed.

You proved – all of you – that your grassroots effort to save your company and harness thousands and thousands of people was not about a family conflict or a Greek tragedy, but more about fairness, justice and a solid moral compass that unites the human soul.

I have always believed that we are born into this world and at a certain place to be with certain people for a

251

reason and a purpose. Everyone has a destiny, and because of you, I stand here with a renewed vigor and a sense of purpose. May we always remember this past summer first as a time where our collective values of loyalty and courage and kindness for one another really prevailed. And, in that process, we just happened to save our company. As you gave generously to those who had less than you, the public watched in awe and admiration, because you empowered others to seek change. You all have demonstrated to the world that it is a person's moral obligation and social responsibility to protect the culture which provides an honorable and dignified place in which to work ...

It's a wonderful speech. Arthur T spoke to his people with paternal pride, rather like a father who acknowledges that today his children have all grown up – and even gone beyond him – and this has made him very proud and humble. He used the 'you' pronoun as a gesture of respect for the efforts and success of the workers, occasionally switching back to 'we' and 'I'. But it was when Arthur spoke of his own father that the emotion really kicked in:

My father would be so very proud of each and every one of you, and especially proud of the pride that you all possess.

As Arthur spoke of his father, the audience called out, 'WE LOVE YOU!'

Arthur replied:

I love you all!

Then he said:

*Let's take that pride and let's move forward doing what
we love to do ...*

The speech made a broad transition through its changing
pronouns, almost re-enacting the power shift that had just
taken place. The workers had demonstrated not just their
loyalty, but also their strength and purpose. Now it seemed that
both Arthur and his staff had grown up and grown strong and
they would move forward together. No more paternalism, only
solidarity and community.

How to make a one-liner

Here's another danger for the novice speechwriter, and one of
the biggest threats to the voice of reason. It is not uncommon
for the media team to urge you to come up with a catch-phrase
or tag line – or suggest one themselves – with the aim of creating
the headline that stays in the audience's mind. They will want
you to start with this tag line and then write *towards* it. But if
you are seeking to be the voice of reason, then the great lines
can only arise naturally as a summation of logical argument. It
just doesn't work the other way around.

But even when, as a responsible speechwriter, you seek to avoid cheap slogans, it's still possible to write, inadvertently, a tag line that is so catchy it potentially derails the speech. To counter this risk, I developed a very effective relationship with one member of a client's media team. He would read my drafts carefully. Whatever he might have thought about them, he never presumed to tell me directly what was wrong. (This was wise, because in those days I was almost irrationally oversensitive to spin-doctor interference.) Rather, he would simply suggest to me what he thought the likely headline might be. That line might well have been the most vivid and interesting in the speech. It might even have been my favourite. But if it was distracting or detracting from the main theme, it had to go.

And then there are the times when just the right line arises organically out of the text and spirit of a speech. In 2000, I worked on a speech for Frank Sartor, the Lord Mayor of Sydney, as he welcomed the Olympic Torch on the steps of Sydney Town Hall after its journey around the world and Australia. On that steamy night, my husband and I went into the city and found ourselves at the back of a crowd of over 100,000 people watching the Lord Mayor greet golfer Karrie Webb as she jogged towards him down George Street, dressed in white and proudly holding aloft the sleek silver object blazing with light.

The Lord Mayor's remarks were brief, ending with a line that only popped into my head as I was about to finish and send my draft, and perhaps drawn from my own childlike excitement about the Olympics:

CRAFTING WORDS THAT CONNECT

From now on, Sydney is open 24 hours a day!

The mob roared with bacchanalian delight.

The biggest speech I ever worked on for Kim Beazley was an address to the National Press Club in October 1995 at the launch of a booklet called 'The Labor Party Achievements Document'. The Keating Labor government was preparing itself for an election that it was very likely to lose, in which case Beazley was almost certain to take over as Labor leader of the opposition. The speech was a pre-election pitch to rally the Labor faithful. It was also a first draft of the history of the Hawke–Keating era, and a unifying platform that he would later work from as the next Labor leader.

The speech was thoroughgoing and serious, listing all the ways in which Australia would be worse off under a Howard Liberal government. But it needed a hit of energy, vigour and humour – and while I can do wit, broad political comedy is not my strength. So we asked author and part-time Labor speechwriter, Bob Ellis, to read the draft and suggest a line or two. You won't find it difficult to spot Ellis's larrikin wit in the following:

> *On gaining office in 1983, Labor took on the challenge of fixing the ramshackle economy left behind by successive conservative governments. The conservatives had taken Australia out of the mainstream of economic and social progress that was occurring in other industrialised countries. Our benchmark economies in the OECD were going past us; but still the conservatives did nothing*

to help win back our place among the leading nations.
Where Australia had, for more than a century, been a
world leader in social and political progress, conservative
governments had taken Australia backward. Under the
conservatives, the Australian economy had crawled under
the lino and put its toes in its ears.

Ellis's chaotically hilarious last line was, of course, the grab on the evening news. And while it was certainly funny, it came out of the reasoned argument of the speech. Ellis created the grab that was a natural extension of the line of thinking the rest of the speech had explored.

Sometimes when people quote from the great speeches of history they forget that the most memorable lines are almost always a form of summing up, a product of the very process of writing the speech.

Case study

Great lines arise from strong arguments:
Prime Minister Ben Chifley in 1949 and
President Abraham Lincoln in 1861

Australian post-war prime minister Ben Chifley's 'Light on the Hill' speech was delivered on 12 June 1949 to the New South Wales Branch of the Australian Labor Party. If you have ever looked it up on various modern websites, you might get the impression that the entire speech was just 484 words long. Wrong. It was around 3300 words long, and those frequently cited 484 words constitute the final few paragraphs (or 'peroration', in rhetoric speak).

The context of Chifley's speech was that he was a leader under siege, doing the hard work of post-World War II reconstruction, against enormous internal and external odds, in order to lay the foundations for Australia to become the successful, moderate, prosperous, multicultural society it is today.

Here's what Chifley addressed in his 3300 words. He calmly downplayed the odds of a new world war against Russia. He argued against the merits of Communism, which was a threat within his own party and a scourge within the unions. He outlined the enormous economic problems facing the world, and especially Europe, with massive shortages of all kinds of basic resources. He spoke about the want and deprivation in Asia, concurrent with a population explosion. He explained the worldwide currency and trade crisis – with the US dollar so strong against the British sterling economies that trade imbalances were inhibiting recovery. He argued on the grounds of humanity and self-interest the need for Australia to keep exporting wool, wheat, butter and meat to the UK, despite the relatively poor economic returns. He talked about the huge opportunities that existed for Australia, and about his government's program of growth, investment and expansion. He chided the private sector for its continued complaints when his government was doing so much to support it. He emphasised the duty and national self-interest involved in bringing displaced peoples to Australia from Europe to build our post-war nation. He told the unions they must accept his immigration program while he would continue to support existing labour conditions. He heavied the miners' union, which was threatening to strike (and, in fact, soon did), stressing the concessions that had already been made and talking up the need for energy to fuel the post-war reconstruction program.

Chifley's speech grappled truthfully and in detail with immensely difficult, real-world problems. And then came his final words, when the tone changed and he became reflective and very personal:

I have had the privilege of leading the Labor Party for nearly four years. They have not been easy times and it has not been an easy job. It is a man-killing job and would be impossible if it were not for the help of my colleagues and members of the movement. No Labor minister or leader ever has an easy job. The urgency that rests behind the Labor movement, pushing it on to do things, to create new conditions, to reorganize the economy of the country, always means that the people who work within the Labor movement, people who lead, can never have an easy job. The job of the evangelist is never easy. Because of the turn of fortune's wheel your Premier and I have gained some prominence in the Labor movement. But the strength of the movement cannot come from us. We may make plans and pass legislation to help and direct the economy of the country. But the job of getting the things the people of the country want comes from the roots of the Labor movement – the people who support it.

When I sat at a Labor meeting in the country with only 10 or 15 men there, I found a man sitting beside me who had been working in the Labor movement for 54 years. I have no doubt that many of you have been doing the same, not hoping for any advantage from the movement, not hoping for personal gain, but because you believe in a movement that has been built up to bring better conditions to the people. Therefore the success of the Labor Party at the next election depends entirely, as it always has done, on the people who work.

I try to think of the Labor movement, not as putting an extra sixpence into somebody's pocket, or making somebody Prime Minister or Premier, but as a movement bringing something better to the people, better standards of living, greater happiness to the mass of the people.

We have a great objective – the light on the hill – which we aim to reach by working for the betterment of mankind not only here but anywhere we may give a helping hand. If it were not for that, the Labor movement would not be worth fighting for.

If the movement can make someone more comfortable, give someone a greater feeling of security for their children, a feeling that if a depression comes there will be work, that the government is striving its hardest to do its best, then the Labor movement will be completely justified. It does not matter about persons like me who

have our limitations. I only hope that the generosity,
kindliness and friendliness shown to me by thousands of
my colleagues in the Labor movement will continue to be
given to the movement and add zest to its work.

After reading the full speech and learning all that he was dealing with, you understand the weariness behind Chifley's closing words. And the loneliness. The trials of leadership during the war had already killed his predecessor and friend John Curtin. Chifley himself was to die exactly two years after giving this speech, in June 1951, having lost an election.

Could Chifley have written these beautiful 484 words without the 2800 tough, reasoned words that came before it? Of course not. Would they have had the same resonance without those prior words, without their evidence of his thoughtfulness, dedication and effort? Again, no. The final words have an accumulated power precisely because of their place in the totality of Chifley's speech, with all its intelligence, grit, detail, determination and sincerity.

Another example of this can be found in US President Abraham Lincoln's First Inaugural Address, written in the shadow of a looming civil war. Many remember the final words of that speech – the lyrical appeal for peace:

I am loath to close. We are not enemies, but friends. We
must not be enemies. Though passion may have strained
it must not break our bonds of affection. The mystic
chords of memory, stretching from every battlefield

and patriot grave to every living heart and hearthstone
all over this broad land, will yet swell the chorus of the
Union, when again touched, as surely they will be, by the
better angels of our nature.

But if you take the time to read the foregoing 3500 words, you will see that they are as tough, clear, reasoned and legal-minded as you might expect from any black-letter lawyer debating what was essentially, at that stage, a legal issue. Indeed, Lincoln originally intended to close his address with the unsparing question: 'Shall it be peace or sword?' That softer ending, so beloved today, was prompted by his secretary of state William Seward. I have no doubt Lincoln was only prepared to include the famous ending because he was satisfied that he had fully laid out the necessary hard truths in the previous paragraphs.

If you are a professional speechwriter, you are guaranteed to come across spin-doctors, media advisers and other experts who will demand you ignore the 'difficult issues' altogether and just 'focus on the positive'. If you thoughtlessly comply – if you cut out the first 3000 words in order to concentrate on the high-blown peroration – you are no longer a speechwriter, just a third-rate propagandist. And anyway, it won't work. If you are looking to be the voice of reason, never underestimate your audience, or try to trick them, or bamboozle them, or distract them from the truth. You must insist on the merits of facts, argument and reason, and you do so out of respect for yourself and your audience. And because it works.

Drafting wars

When you leaf through your anthology of famous speeches – admiring the words of Lincoln or Churchill or Martin Luther King Jr or Nelson Mandela – you'll find yourself swept along by the seamless power of great oratory. What you won't discover, unless you carefully investigate the backstory behind each speech, are the conflicts and compromises that were inevitably part of the creative process. Any great speech must overcome the problems involved in its own creation; its authors can only hope that the seams and scars are well disguised.

As a speechwriter, you can get to the end of the first draft and feel completely depleted, and relieved. *There it is*, you say to yourself, *done. It's not the Gettysburg, but it ain't half bad.* But you are not done at all. Some of the hardest work still lies ahead.

There are three things you have yet to manage before you have completed the process:

1. The changes your speaker wants.
2. The changes their underlings advise.
3. The changes you'd like to make yourself.

Passions and proprietary feelings run high in speechwriting, and nowhere more so than in the West Wing of the White House. In *White House Ghosts*, Robert Schlesinger tracks the sneaky means that US presidential speechwriters have adopted in order to get their ideas to the forefront, and keep them there:

- Hanging on to their draft until the last possible minute so their colleagues in Congress did not have time to lobby for major changes.

- Creating an entire dummy draft to circulate to the bureaucrats to keep them distracted while the real speech was worked on in private.

- Inserting key lines over and over again into a draft, on the basis that at least one iteration of the line would not get the red pen. (I have found that to be a very useful tip.)

- Leaking advance copies to the media to make changes impossible.

- When all else fails, using their superior writing skills to send witty and derisive memos arguing against the dullards' changes. (Ronald Reagan's speechwriter Peggy Noonan wasn't averse to this tactic of inspired intellectual bullying.)

Sometimes etiquette is a problem. It's not easy to tell a very senior person – say, the departmental secretary, chief financial officer or chief operating officer – that they have a tin ear and no communications judgement whatsoever. Although I have certainly done so. I don't necessarily recommend this course of action to speechwriters with mortgages.

On wiser days, I have been known to nod and say thank you for a suggestion and then simply 'forget' to incorporate it into the draft. One executive saw successive rounds of a speech and would appear at my desk intermittently, wondering why I hadn't yet included his buzzword in the text. Funnily enough, I never, ever remembered.

Another time, the interfering executive wasn't particularly senior, but he was a longstanding friend and colleague of the CEO. The CEO asked me to do my best to accommodate his friend and give him a role in the drafting process. I wrote a 2500-word speech. The colleague came back with 6000 words of his own. I tried in vain to find something of value in any of them. I went back to him with the original draft plus a few polite paragraphs containing some of his language and ideas. He came back with another 4000 words. This went on until the day before delivery, when the speaker abandoned the bonds of friendship and gave the slightly modified original 20-minute speech.

I have been lucky enough to work with many confident leaders who've had a strong sense of what would work for them in a speech, but also been happy to entertain the suggestions in my drafts around language and narrative. Each side makes its case, learns things, gives way a little and gets pretty good results. In the end, the speaker always owns the speech, and his or her wishes must be respected.

Okay, not always.

There was one particular chair who reviewed the draft of a short speech and had his personal assistant send it back to me with many unflattering marginal remarks and proposed changes. This would have been fine, except that if I had included all his edits it would have changed the tone of the speech, inflaming a sensitive issue connected with a state government. So I sought out the communications manager in some despair. He calmly went online, opened my draft speech, incorporated just five of the chair's most minor edits into the draft, and then printed out the document. The stroke of genius lay in his final step. With a flourish, he ran his yellow highlighter pen over great swathes of text adjacent to those minor changes so it looked as though the speech had been drastically amended in accord with the chair's wishes. In fact, there had been no substantive change at all.

'There!' said the communications manager, delightedly, as he scanned the document and emailed it back to the chair. 'He will take a quick look and see that his edits have been incorporated.' The manager was quite right. Back came the chair's feedback: a satisfied, 'Much better.'

Then there are the peers, colleagues, consultants and other secondary parties to the speech-drafting process. I confess some rather unfortunate aspects of my personality have been on display when I've been pushed to the very limits of tolerance by silly edits on a tight deadline. Shouting may have happened. Also rudeness. I may have actually said, loudly, 'GO AWAY!' I can only say in my defence that part of my post-speech routine is to figure out who I need to thank for their help, and to whom I may need to offer an apology.

There is, of course, the distinct possibility that the critics have a point. There may well be something wrong in the text that a clumsy edit is trying to fix. So rather than just accepting or rejecting someone's red-pen mark-ups, I encourage people to explain to me exactly why they have a problem with the language. If I understand the underlying concern, then I can make the appropriate corrections. It matters, because sometimes a change in one part of a speech can alter the balance of the whole thing, and I need to be alert to the need for wider amendments.

Finally, there is the most annoying, critical and pernickety judge of all: me. Serious speechwriters never stop working on a speech until it is delivered. And sometimes even afterwards. Back in the 1st century BCE, Cicero assiduously revised his own political and courtroom speeches before publication. This was wise – and it clearly worked, given that we are still reading them 2000 years later.

Another version-control issue occurs when the speechwriter decides to make her own last-minute changes to the speech. As I have discovered to my cost, this can cause major problems in the multi-platform instantaneous digital age. If you are writing a speech for a major company announcement, you will have a media press release, the company website, Twitter, Facebook, staff briefing packs and talking points, letters to clients and who knows how many more communications all echoing the key points of the speech. This wide dissemination is one reason why a great speech is such a valuable investment: it becomes a driving and unifying communication tool. That's also why it's so important that the final version of the text be accurately dispersed through the system.

I once nearly lost a valued friendship with a first-rate internal communications manager when, with the CEO, I kept making changes to a major draft speech right up until lodgement with the stock exchange an hour before delivery – and forgot to use track-changes. I was sending this poor woman multiple revised versions of a 25-minute speech, without any mark-up, in which she had to figure out for herself what had changed before sharing it with her stressed-out team operating across multiple platforms. Afterwards, there was another apology from me. This time a long one.

Although version management can be incredibly exhausting, a good speechwriter has no choice but to fight for the very best possible speech, right up until the moment of its delivery. In defence of the best version of a story, a speechwriter sometimes has to be a warrior too.

Words and ethics

I conclude this section with some words about words. It's a sad fact that even a university education in the humanities no longer automatically teaches us how to write well. Most academic writing is turgid and obscure, and when I am teaching rhetoric to university students I find myself guiltily advising them *not* to read academic treatises, at least not if they want to develop a good style in the real world. But more broadly the English language has become debased, because, as George Orwell pointed out in 1946, 'if thought corrupts language, language can also corrupt thought'. The great Australian speechwriter

Don Watson has written several books attacking the corruption of language in Australia, reserving particular loathing for the 'weasel words' of modern corporate jargon.

In the United Kingdom, the writer David Cornwell, better known as John le Carré, echoed these sentiments with his usual uncluttered elegance when he wrote in *The Guardian* on 2 July 2017 of the deleterious impact of President Donald Trump on good communication:

> *In the extraordinary period we are living through – may it be short-lived – it's impossible not to marvel at every contradictory or unintelligible utterance issuing from across the Atlantic. And in marvelling, we come face-to-face with the uses and abuses of language itself.*
>
> *Clear language – lucid, rational language – to a man at war with both truth and reason, is an existential threat. Clear language to such a man is a direct assault on his obfuscations, contradictions and lies. To him, it is the voice of the enemy. To him, it is fake news. Because he knows, if only intuitively, what we know to our cost: that without clear language, there is no standard of truth.*

Cornwell draws for us the inexorable link between words and ethics. I learned to write well in Canberra in the late 1980s, when I was working in the Prime Minister's Department. There I had access to the classified reports of the Office of National Assessments (ONA), an elite agency set up by Prime Minister Malcolm Fraser in the 1970s as an independent source of intelligence advice for the prime minister. The ONA modelled its writing style on *The Economist* magazine: it was simple, declaratory and disdainful of all bureaucratic doublespeak. This style became the unofficial template for all the best foreign-policy writing in the Australian Public Service. I remember the thrill I experienced reading the ONA reports when I found you could cut a long sentence in half and start anew with 'but' or 'and' or 'so' – or, even more daringly, 'because'. It was a gift to a future speechwriter to discover you could write short and readable lines without sacrificing complexity or argument.

Sometimes you will find in bureaucratic and corporate circles that the need for brevity is (perhaps unconsciously) used as a justification for jargon. It is, after all, faster to say 'customer-centric approach' than it is to say 'an approach that puts customers first'. But the point is not how long it takes to write or read the words on the page, or even how long it takes the speaker to say them. The point is how long it takes a human mind to receive, process and accept the words. Quite often, the longer jargon-free form is the shortest route to shared human understanding.

One of the temptations for the novice speechwriter is to make a speech dense and 'writerly'. But a good speech is a natural, true and human thing; it is not constrained and tight. When you are starting out, however, if you write a natural, true and human draft, you may panic because it appears alarmingly simple and basic on the page. Even if you are pleased with the draft yourself, you fear that your superiors will deem you devoid of substance. But you have to push through that fear, because simplicity is the language of leadership.

This clarity of writing, though, is about more than just a modern and mobile style. It is a form of ethics. You take a position and present your point of view so that all the lines of argument can be readily understood and, therefore, questioned or contested. The great cry against jargon and obfuscation is, at its root, a cry for a better, more honest society.

7

Stand and deliver

A SPEECH HAPPENS NOW, at the moment of its delivery. That's what gives this seemingly outdated communication mode its shiver of risk and suspense. And audiences still turn up for speeches because there is always the faint possibility of grand history in the making. Or maybe just a gaffe. A surprise revelation. An unguarded ad-lib. An unexpected audience intervention. *What will the speaker say? What will happen? How will we all react? What will it mean?*

The speechwriter is always the official custodian of the words in any enterprise, and I have often felt like their last lone defender too. So I have been known to heavily downplay the performance aspect of any speech. I may have even been heard to mutter under my breath to a nervous speaker, 'Oh, for God's sake, just get up there and say the damn words.'

That's because I am quite sure that, if they are good enough, the words will do their job. And you won't be surprised to learn that for me the quality of the words is by far the most important aspect of oratory. Abraham Lincoln had a famously high-pitched voice. Isaiah Berlin, 20th-century scholar and political philosopher, used to gabble his public addresses at top speed. Clearly, not a fatal flaw. And absolutely not a primary issue when you are in the business of making history.

And yet ...

There's nothing grander than a speaker in full command of themselves and their audience. And there is nothing more moving or exhilarating than a great speech, well delivered. Also, it has to be said that the delivery of a speech is often no longer confined to the immediate audience, but filmed or recorded and posted online for all the world to see. So it's not just the words that live on, but the delivery of those words as well.

Politicians tend to have practised public speaking from a very young age. Debating is a great training ground, and so is the floor of the parliament. Traditional political campaigning is all about grassroots speechmaking, usually involving delivery of the same stump speech over and over again, while coping with heckling, yawning, abuse and the odd cream pie. Some politicians can still speak off the cuff with ease, although many younger politicians who have come up through the backrooms tend to lack that oratorical power.

But increasingly, politicians and CEOs seem unable to deliver a powerful set-piece address. A friend with excellent political connections once told me a story that made me laugh with horror. We were discussing the fact that the then leader of the opposition was absolutely failing to connect with the Australian electorate. His public presentations, we agreed, were insipid, his language was dull, his energy levels seemed low. That man sure needed help.

'He's *getting* help,' said my friend, with an ironic smile. 'I saw the marked-up copy of his speech for the Press Club. It had all these dashes and bolded words to indicate pauses and emphasis.' At this point, my friend began guffawing. 'So it was exactly the same old schlock, except that every now and then he would shout a random word, like "PEOPLE!" or "GROWTH!"

'Even worse,' my friend went on, 'one of his staffers told me that the presentation skills guru coached him to move his body in certain ways while speaking to "make him more dynamic". So there he was delivering his speech, when suddenly he would turn to the side and extend one arm to the audience, and one up and behind like some vaudeville performer about to start tap dancing. It was weird.'

As I mentioned in Chapter 3, business leaders come to the task of speechmaking with a very different background to politicians. Yet they are just as integral to our modern society and economy, and they need to be able to speak well and confidently in public. But often they don't. Perhaps this is why, all too often, the communications people collude to protect the CEO from this stressful and sometimes unpleasant duty. The communicators themselves may not fully understand that sometimes there is simply no substitute for a speech. I can't count how many times people have suggested to me that a leader would be better off talking off the cuff, or from a few jotted notes, or on a panel, or in a question-and-answer session with a journalist. Anything, it seems – anything! – but give a 20-minute speech in which their head is down over the page and they stumble their way clumsily through the lines.

But it doesn't have to be this way. It is absolutely possible to protect the integrity of those carefully crafted words *and* connect with an audience.

Ailsa Piper is a highly accomplished writer, speechmaking and acting coach, broadcaster, performer and theatre director, with vast experience working as an actor herself and as a director of other actors. These days she is also focused on writing books. She has taught me a lot about how to give speeches myself, and if she can help *me*, then I have no doubt even the least confident CEO could quickly improve their performance if they cared to do so. At the risk of oversimplifying Ailsa Piper's vast knowledge, here are some of the things I've learned from her:

1. Rehearse. Aloud.
2. It's okay not to perform.
3. Visualise how you will begin the speech.
4. Use the layout of the speech to help.
5. Use your natural voice. And breathe.

Rehearse. Aloud.

In fact, record yourself delivering your speech on your phone. Or get someone to record it for you. Play your speech back to yourself as you go for your morning walk or run. Listen to it as you move. You don't even need to think about it particularly. And if you only have time to listen to it once, that's absolutely fine. The body will take in the rhythm of the speech and give you an awareness of what is coming and when, and how long each section will take to deliver.

The goal is to take the speech into your body, so that when it comes time to give the speech, the muscle memory will take over. It means that with comparatively little preparation, you will have a very strong understanding of the cartography of the speech, its shape, its rhythms, its rise and fall. You won't need to have your head down trying to work out where you are.

It's okay *not* to perform.

Many excellent leaders are introverts. They don't feel at all comfortable prowling around the stage with a headset, or gesticulating wildly, or using cheesy props. Plenty of extroverted CEOs feel exactly the same. The good news is that in speeches, big gestures aren't at all necessary. The judicious use of *small* gestures can be equally powerful. A finger in the air can work beautifully – as long as it punctuates the right point in the speech.

Here's another thought: in theatre and film, the dominant figure – whether it's the King or the Godfather – is often static. Power equates to stillness; it's those who are in subservient positions who are moving around.

When we think of high-energy, active CEOs, they tend to be entrepreneurs such as Richard Branson or Steve Jobs who genuinely personify the dynamic values of their brand. But most corporate CEOs are different to this, and will be better served by going with a more natural and low-key style. It's absolutely okay not to move about, and to trust that a few deliberate but small gestures can still have great power.

If you do nothing else, visualise how you will begin the speech.

A lot can happen in those first moments as you take yourself to the podium that will forge an electric connection between you and the audience.

When you get in front of your audience, stop and look. Embrace the audience with your gaze. They want you to like them. Take them in. Love them a little, even.

And importantly, let them take *you* in too. How you look interests them. Don't be afraid of it. They want to learn your cues, your gestures, your style. You might even fiddle with your papers or take a drink to stretch out this moment. It's a little bit tense, isn't it? It's a little bit dramatic too. This is drama, remember? Breathe.

And now something very wonderful starts to happen. Before you have even said a word, before you have even exhaled that breath, the audience is leaning in to you.

Use the layout of the speech to help.

More pages with big, easy, readable print will work far better than fewer pages that are dense with words. The audience won't even notice you are turning the page if you are confident, comfortable and giving them regular eye contact. They absolutely *will* notice if you are scrolling your eyes down a too-long page to find where you are up to.

In Chapter 4, I referred to Hilary Benn's speech to the British Parliament in December 2015, in which he supported the proposition that Britain should fight against Islamic State in Syria. It was an extraordinary performance to watch, applauded at the time and celebrated afterwards. Benn quite openly used a very large-print text, turning the pages rapidly as he delivered his address. But reading from the text did not hinder his performance. Made confident by having the words before him, and knowing where he was in the speech because of the large print, he could turn his head, move his arms, make eye contact with his friends and opponents, and appear completely at ease.

Use your natural voice. And breathe.

Use the power of the visible breath. That slightly theatrical intake of breath between sections is a real lean-in moment. The shift in tone or subject. The shared silence. The silent comment on what has gone before.

I found this suggestion quite life-changing. It was especially useful to me because the usual blanket advice I had received about the delivery of my own speeches was a generic injunction to 'slow down'. Well, I don't talk like Winston Churchill. It would be absurd for me to try to do so. For me to slow down noticeably would be stilted and awkward and unnatural. I would sound like someone trying to sound like an orator. It would make me nervous. But I discovered I could deploy Ailsa's advice to accentuate the natural pauses between thoughts. That way, I didn't have to slow down the words; rather, I simply lengthened the significant breaths between.

One way to help you remember to do this is to openly insert the words 'STOP' or 'BREATHE' when you get to the end of a key section of your text, or just before introducing a new one. And don't just take a breath, think of it as taking a *visible* breath. One that the audience can see. That beat is important. It gives the audience a rest too, and a cue to prepare for something new and different.

Here's a final thought from my own experience. If you have a good speech, then the great joy is that you can just forget about yourself as you deliver it. The occasion stops being about you, and starts being all about the gift you are bringing to the audience – whether it's information, inspiration, solace or joy. If you feel nervous before you give a speech, have a think about whether it's because you are going to waste people's time with another boring, clichéd, hackneyed piece of prose. When you have a good speech, when you have something you really want to say, and it's true and you believe it, then what you look like and how your voice sounds really become unimportant. It stops being about you, and starts being about the communication.

Believe your words, craft them, own them. Then share them out loud.

Strategies for women speakers

I have been writing speeches for many years – and you won't be surprised to learn that the majority of my clients are men. But I've also worked with quite a few women in leadership roles. A disproportionate number of them have been country girls who grew up in regional or rural Australia: hardy, self-confident, pragmatic, no-nonsense, good-humoured women. Each one of them has had to fight harder than any man for the power she has attained and kept (and I have often felt like the oversensitive inner-city writer in their formidable presence).

Is giving speeches different for women? A while back I had a conversation with an emerging business leader who is in huge demand as a speech-giver for corporations and conferences. Unlike most of my female corporate clients, however, she is not naturally extroverted. She has put herself into the public domain because she knows she must be a public figure if she wants to influence the future.

Here is a list of what she saw as some of the unstated and implicit rules for business women in public:

· Women can't boast or swagger. On the other hand, they shouldn't be too modest or self-deprecating.
· Women can't be funny. They shouldn't try jokes.
· Women can't use too much emotion because that will make them look weak.
· Women can't use too much reason because then they'll seem cold and hard.
· Women can't ever be aggressive, and even appearing argumentative can be a problem.

I think she's right. Basically, just think of all the legitimate fears that men have about public speaking, then double them. That is what it feels like to be an emerging woman leader speaking in public.

Then there's the inevitable focus on appearance. A woman speaker has to know that her 'sex appeal' will be carefully appraised. Body language is policed. Women can't move their legs or stretch their arms. Even the voice must be tamed. High-pitched voices – just normal women's voices – aren't acceptable.

So what can women do to break free of these limitations? The strategy that an older generation has used with some success has been to tough it out, conforming to the broad expectations of female appearance while working hard to change the underlying assumptions. For example, I have worked with business leader Ann Sherry at various times in her corporate career and watched her develop as a leader over many years. She is completely comfortable in herself. She has an infectious grin, a down-to-earth style, and an absolutely modern and sensible approach to how workplaces should function. I have also worked with Margaret Jackson, former Qantas chair, who is super-smart and, more than any other leader I have worked with, has had the confidence and breadth to talk about her personal experiences and emotions in public. Both Sherry and Jackson are admirable and effective leaders. Neither of them ever went on about the hardships and challenges of being a woman in business. They just put on their power suits, squared their padded shoulders and found a way to make the rules work for them.

But I don't think this approach will work for younger women, nor should it. I think the time to hope that the rules will evolve naturally has well and truly gone. So my advice to younger women is *not* to make the timid compromises necessary to be deemed acceptable. Know that the rules are there, and that they are stupid. And chuck them. Overcome them. Overturn them. If we all stopped playing by rules that are stupid, then those rules would quickly crumble. Make your jokes, admit your weaknesses, boast about your accomplishments, wear whatever the hell you like, don't try to deepen your voice, don't give a damn about a few extra kilos, take up a lot of space, and generally act like you own the joint.

Women need to take their cue from all the fantastic performers who have shown that women in comedy can be funny, smart and silly; fat, thin and in between; political, switched-on and argumentative – women like Tina Fey and Amy Schumer and Rebel Wilson and Judith Lucy and Jane Turner and many more. And to take heart from the women leading the #MeToo and #TimesUp movements. The time is ripe for women leaders with the confidence to own their own voices wholeheartedly. It's a historic shift and a historic opportunity.

But that doesn't make it easy. It is really tough for women in business and politics. All the women I know in leadership roles have had to put up with a lot. This will continue until women achieve leadership roles in sufficient numbers for us to be taken for granted. I want to see more and more women walking up to the podium, taking up the space, grabbing the moment and having their say.

When Anna Bligh was premier of Queensland, she found herself one summer having to manage the most extraordinary sequence of natural disasters – floods, hurricanes, more floods. She made it her business to brief the media and the public every few hours about the rapidly changing situation. She would appear on television with a barely ironed shirt, no makeup and roughly brushed hair. She was too busy leading to worry about that stuff.

Emma González has emerged as the most charismatic of the group of astounding students from Marjory Stoneman Douglas High School in Florida that is campaigning for gun control in America following the massacre at their school. In the days immediately following the mass shooting, a shaven-headed, weeping González delivered a riveting and rousing speech that electrified the world: 'We are up here standing together because if all our government and President can do is send thoughts and prayers, then it's time for victims to be the change that we need to see.'

Rosie Batty became Australian of the Year in 2015. Out of profound personal tragedy – the murder of her son by her former partner – she became a powerful advocate for better approaches to the problem of domestic violence.

These women have had the courage to let go of ego and self-preservation in pursuit of greater causes. If you want to lead, you have to persuade. If you want to persuade, then you will need to give speeches. I want to see more women with the impulse to lead, and the self-belief undoubtedly required of them to do it. I admire people who want to be leaders, and I take great pride in helping the good ones. May more and more of them be women!

Summing up (with PJK)

MANY PEOPLE are in so-called leadership positions, but are not leaders. As you are reading this line, you are already conjuring up an image of someone you know who has the leadership title but isn't genuinely fulfilling the role. They are the ones who don't take the risks demanded by leadership. Instead, they choose to do very little, which it is all too easy to get away with. To attempt no reform means the leader doesn't have to convince anyone of anything. They can just sit back and take the money. They can twirl in their leather chairs and work out how to invest their enormous paycheques. Which raises the question: how does a person in a leadership position become a leader? How do they make themselves matter?

I got one answer to this question back in 2003. Allan Gyngell, my former boss at the Department of the Prime Minister and

Cabinet, and one of my formative writing teachers, had gone on to become the adviser on international relations to Prime Minister Paul Keating (PJK). After the Labor government lost the 1996 election, Gyngell had stayed with him and supported him in a variety of ways, including helping him with speeches. When Gyngell was appointed the first executive director of the Lowy Institute for International Affairs, he thought Keating might find it useful to have someone in his office, at least for the interim, and recommended me. As it turned out, Keating didn't need my help for anything, and I only spent a few memorable weeks in the lamp-lit treasure house that was his office.

One day PJK stopped by my desk. 'Luv, would you like to sit in on this meeting I've got? He's an ASEAN leader on an official visit.'

The South East Asian guest was a celebrity who had entered politics late and become a senator. I speculated that he had formerly been an actor or journalist – one of those TV-friendly types. He certainly looked pleased with himself and very relaxed. He was all courtesy and charm to Australia's former prime minister.

This senator had been on most of his official calls by now, and had probably been told by think-tanks and ministers and senators how important his country was to Australia, how well it was doing, and how we all looked forward to closer relations. It seemed at first that this interview would proceed just like the others, without incident, and the senator would go off to a nice lunch and feel satisfied with his charm offensive.

But this was PJK.

Suddenly, the former prime minister leaned forward. 'It's terrible what's happening in your country,' he said. 'The poverty! And it's all so unnecessary.'

It was almost comical. The visitor's smooth face simply cracked open. Just for a second. Then the TV training kicked in. He pulled it together into a smile. But clearly no one had warned him that things could go like this.

It got worse. The Keating hands were rotating softly in the air, as if directing an imaginary orchestra.

'You know, the system anywhere, it just ticks over, it runs itself. Left alone, nothing will change. But if you want to be in politics, it's all about change. Isn't it?'

I could see this idea of civic leadership had never occurred to the celebrity senator. His smile got even tauter.

But next to me, something else was happening. The senator's adviser had been sitting – as advisers must do, as indeed I was – square and silent. I had already noticed his sad eyes. But as Keating started talking, I could sense a shift. The adviser leaned ever so slightly forward. He began minutely adjusting his body as if it were a radar trying to get the best reception for an important message.

'And what's the point of public life,' the former prime minister was saying, 'with all its drawbacks, unless you are out to do something, unless you make the place better?'

Now the adviser was on the edge of his seat. I could feel the heat emanating from him.

Then PJK began juggling the Australian economy with those feline hands. He outlined the way his government had taken Australia from being an industrial museum to today's stronger, better, more open Australia. But he stressed that it had taken an enormous effort of intellect and persuasion.

'Only takes one person,' said PJK, looking meaningfully at the senator, and no doubt recalling his own genius.

The celebrity politician rose and left with all possible haste. But the adviser, with his deep and passionate eyes, lingered a moment and we warmly shook hands.

He came in close to me. 'When we had the dictator,' he said, in a voice full of emotion, 'I was there, marching in the streets. We had to fight so hard. Now we must, we must make something better for ourselves.'

He followed his boss out, and I watched Australia's former prime minister retreat to his office.

I look back on that small scene and I wonder why it still means so much to me. Of course, there is the unmatched charisma of Paul Keating. I remember how thrilled I was to see that he still felt such passion for the potential of civic life.

But I remember that scene particularly because of the adviser. Here was a man like me, someone who wanted to find a good leader and help that leader create a better world. I've been so lucky to do that in Australia, working with some great leaders in business and government.

Paul Keating used to say, 'Change the government, change the country.' He was quite right. For better or worse, leaders matter.

When things were going badly for Athens in the long war with Sparta, and at a time when the community was highly critical of his leadership, Pericles, the great citizen-statesman,

summoned the assembly and berated his fellow citizens for
their complaints. He gave it to them straight:

*You, in your private afflictions, are angry with me that
I persuaded you to declare war. Therefore you are angry
also with yourselves, that you voted with me.*

He went on:

*You took me to be what I think I am, superior to
most in foresight, in oratorical ability – for if a man
cannot explain himself clearly, he might as well have no
foresight – in patriotism, and in personal honesty ...*

Foresight, oratory, patriotism, personal honesty: the four
qualities of the Greek statesman then, and of the great
statesman today. Even the decision to try to persuade others
through reasoned speech is a contribution to a more democratic
society, one that is underpinned by freedom of speech, political
equality and the rule of law.

Pericles went on to say this:

*Our public men have, besides politics, their private
affairs to attend to, and our ordinary citizens, though
occupied with the pursuits of industry, are still good
judges of public matters; for unlike any other nation,
we regard him who takes no part in these duties not as
unambitious – but as useless.*

Oh, yes. And this was where Pericles made the point I quoted back in Chapter 1, explaining exactly what he meant by 'useless':

We Athenians may either put forward policy proposals or make assessments of them. We don't regard speeches and policy debate as a stumbling-block to action, we regard them as an indispensable preliminary to choosing the right course.

The speech as an 'indispensable preliminary' to action. That's the core of modern democracies. To the modern mind – now accustomed to outsourcing nearly all aspects of citizenship – perhaps the Greek notion of full participation sounds unduly onerous. But the Greeks firmly believed that your value as a citizen, and indeed as a human being, was defined by your contribution to civic life. They even had a term for the elites of their day who shirked those civic duties: *idiotai* – the source of our English word 'idiots'.

It should come as no surprise that many speechwriters are either professional historians or serious readers of history. They've read enough history to want to make it. They are optimists too, believing the future can be different to and better than the past. The impulse of the speechwriter is undoubtedly to influence people, to persuade them how to think and feel and act. And really, there's no point in writing, or for that matter giving, a speech unless you want to create change in people's minds and hearts.

For those who have power in our modern democracy, it's your privilege and responsibility to make it count. As Paul Keating said in that memorable meeting, echoing Pericles 2400 years earlier, why wouldn't you *want* to make it count?

I conclude by returning to that youthful memory of my dear dad and his unsteady wedding speech, and the hunger I felt in those days to read and hear and write true words. If we care about living together in flourishing societies, we must, today more than ever, listen with generous and open-minded attention to different and opposing points of view. And we'd better take care to tell our truths with all the clarity, integrity and persuasive power that we can muster.

Bibliography

Abdel-Magied, Y, 'As Lionel Shriver made light of identity, I had no choice but to walk out on her', *The Guardian*, 10 September 2016

Albanese, A, 'Government with a Purpose', transcript, address to the National Press Club, 25 January 2012, http://anthonyalbanese.com.au/speech-to-national-press-club-government-with-a-purpose

Aristotle, *Treatise on Rhetoric*, trans. T Buckley, Prometheus Books, New York, 2nd edn, 1995

Beazley, K, 'Many Cultures – One Nation', address to the Federation of Ethnic Communities of Australia 16th Annual Conference, Melbourne, 16 November 1995, author copy

Beazley, K, 'Shaping the Nation', address to the National Press Club, Canberra, 18 October 1995, author copy

Benn, H, 'In Favour of Syrian Air Strikes', address to the British House of Commons, 2 December 2015, https://www.youtube.com/watch?v=m_dRCzd19Uc

Bratton, B H, 'What's Wrong with TED Talks?', address to TEDX San Diego, 30 December 2013, www.youtube.com/watch?v=Yo5cKRmJaf0&vl=en

Cadzow, J, 'What Turned Steve Smith into a Cheat?', *Sydney Morning Herald*, 23 June 2018

Cameron, D, 'The Bloomberg Speech', London, 23 January 2013, www.youtube.com/watch?v=8Ls60Wbq_dk&t=1835s

Chifley, J B, 'Light on the Hill', address to Labor Party Conference, 1949, in A W Stargardt, ed., *Things Worth Fighting For: Speeches by Joseph Benedict Chifley*, Australian Labor Party, Melbourne, 1953, pp 58–65

Churchill, W, 'In this Solemn Hour', transcript, 19 May 1940, www.winstonchurchill.org/resources/speeches/1940-the-finest-hour/be-ye-men-of-valour

Cicero, *On the Ideal Orator*, trans. J M May and J Wisse, Oxford University Press, BCE55/2001

Clark, T, 'Paul Keating's Redfern Park Speech and its Rhetorical Legacy', *Overland*, Edition 213, Summer 2013

Clinton, B, 'Democratic National Convention Speech', 5 September 2012, www.youtube.com/watch?v=uzDhk3BHi6Q

Cornwell, D, 'Why We Should Learn German', *The Guardian*, 2 July 2017

Crean, S, 'You Should Not Be Going', transcript, 23 January 2003, australianpolitics.com/2003/01/23/you-should-not-be-going-crean-to-troops.html

Davis, L, 'New Directions for CRA', address to Securities Institute of Australia, Sydney/Melbourne, March 1995, obtained via personal communication from Rio Tinto head office, London

Davis, L, 'The New Competencies in Mining', address to Australian Institute of Company Directors, Melbourne,

3 October 1995, obtained via personal communication from Rio Tinto head office, London

Demoulas, A, 'Thanks for Your Loyalty', 28 August 2014, www.youtube.com/watch?v=xMIhZrzxjMY

Duhigg, C, *The Power of Habit: Why We Do What We Do in Life and Business*, Random House, New York, 2012

Elizabeth I, 'The Tilbury Speech', British Library transcript, 1588, www.bl.uk/learning/timeline/item102878.html

Freudenberg, G, *A Certain Grandeur: Gough Whitlam in Politics*, Macmillan, Melbourne, 1977

Gillard, J, 'Misogyny Speech', Address to the Australian Parliament, transcript, 9 October 2012, http://parlinfo.aph. gov.au/parlInfo/search/display/display.w3p;query=Id%3A% 22chamber%2Fhansardr%2F5a0ebb6b-c6c8-4a92-ac13- 219423c2048d%2F0039%22

Glover, D, *The Art of Great Speeches: And Why We Remember Them*, Cambridge University Press, Cambridge, 2011

González, E, 'We Call BS', Fort Lauderdale, 17 February 2018, https://www.youtube.com/watch?v=ZxD3o-9H1lY

Heilemann, J, 'The Dog and the Preacher', *New York Magazine*, 7 September 2012

Howard, J, 'Gun Rally, Sale', transcript, 16 June 1996, pmtranscripts.pmc.gov.au/release/transcript-10030

Jobs, S, 'Stanford University Commencement Address', 12 June 2005, www.youtube.com/watch?v=UF8uR6Z6KLc

Jobs, S, 'Truce with Microsoft', MacWorld Boston, 6 August 1997, www.youtube.com/watch?v=almoJa_c_FA

Keating, P, 'On that historic day in Redfern, the words I wrote are mine', *Sydney Morning Herald*, 26 August 2010

Keating, P, 'Redfern Park Speech', transcript, 10 December 1992, antar.org.au/sites/default/files/paul_keating_speech_transcript.pdf

Keating, P, 'Remembrance Day', transcript, 11 November 1993, https://www.awm.gov.au/commemoration/speeches/keating-remembrance-day-1993

Kennedy, J F, 'We Choose to Go to the Moon', transcript, 12 September 1962, https://er.jsc.nasa.gov/seh/ricetalk.htm

King, M L, Jr, 'I Have a Dream', Lincoln Memorial, transcript, 28 August 1963, www.americanrhetoric.com/speeches/mlkihaveadream.htm

Kitto, H D F, *The Greeks*, Penguin, London, 1957

Lamott, A, *Bird by Bird: Some Instructions on Writing and Life*, Anchor, New York, 1995

Langton, M, 'Lecture 3: Old Barriers and New Models: The Private Sector, Government and the Economic Empowerment of Aboriginal Australians', *53rd Boyer Lectures*, ABC Radio, 2 December 2012, www.abc.net.au/radionational/programs/boyerlectures/2012-boyer-lectures/4393916

Lincoln, A, 'Gettysburg Address', transcript, 19 November 1863, www.abrahamlincolnonline.org/lincoln/speeches/gettysburg.htm

Lopate, P, *To Show and to Tell: The Craft of Literary Nonfiction*, Simon & Schuster, New York, 2013

McDonald, D, *The Firm: The Story of McKinsey and its Secret Influence on American Business*, Simon & Schuster, New York, 2013

McGilchrist, I, *All in the Mind*, ABC Radio National, 17 September 2017 http://www.abc.net.au/radionational/programs/allinthemind/the-divided-brain/8895804

McGilchrist, I, *The Master and his Emissary: The Divided Brain and the Making of the Western World*, Yale University Press, London, 2009

Minto, B, *The Pyramid Principle: Logic in Writing and Thinking*, Pitman, London, 1987

Morrison, D, 'Message to Staff', Australian Army, 12 June 2013, www.youtube.com/watch?v=QaqpoeVgr8U

Noonan, P, *What I Saw at the Revolution: A Political Life in the Reagan Era*, Random House, New York, 1990

Nooyi, I, 'Learn, Earn and Return', address to Indian Institute of Management, 9 April 2015, www.youtube.com/watch?v=8U4DdDqulu0

Nooyi, I, 'The Middle Finger', address to Columbia University Business School, transcript, 20 May 2005, www.bloomberg.com/news/articles/2005-05-19/indra-nooyis-graduation-remarks (requires subscription)

O'Neill, P, 'Alcoa Safety Speech', 1987, in C Duhigg, *The Power of Habit: Why We Do What We Do in Life and Business*, Random House, New York, 2012

Obama, B, 'Democratic National Convention Speech', 27 July 2004, www.youtube.com/watch?v=SUU0wXVuvko

Obama, B, 'Democratic National Convention Speech', 7 September 2012, www.youtube.com/watch?v=SUU0wXVuvko

Ogilvy, D, *On Advertising*, Vintage, New York, 1983

Pearson, N, 'Eulogy for Gough Whitlam', transcript, 4 November 2014, http://www.reconciliationsa.org.au/news/reconciliation/read-noel-pearsons-eulogy-for-the-late-former-prime-minister-gough-whitlam

Plattner, M F, 'Is Democracy in Decline?', *Democracy and Society*, Fall–Winter 2016, Vol 13, Issue 1, pp 1–3

Roosevelt, T, 'The Man in the Arena', Paris Sorbonne, transcript, 23 April 1910, www.theodoreroosevelt.com/images/research/speeches/maninthearena.pdf

Rudd, K, 'Apology to Australia's Indigenous Peoples', transcript, 13 February 2008, https://www.australia.gov.au/about-australia/our-country/our-people/apology-to-australias-indigenous-peoples

Schlesinger, R, *White House Ghosts: Presidents and Their Speechwriters*, Simon & Schuster, New York, 2008

Scott, L, 'Twenty First Century Leadership', transcript, 23 October 2005, corporate.walmart.com/_news_/executive-viewpoints/twenty-first-century-leadership

Shriver, L, 'Fiction and Identity Politics', transcript of speech given at the Brisbane Writers' Festival, *The Guardian*, 13 September 2016

Spencer, C, 'Eulogy for Princess Diana', transcript, September 1997, www.bbc.co.uk/news/special/politics97/diana/spencerfull.html

Stone, B, *The Everything Store: Jeff Bezos and the Age of Amazon*, Transworld, London, 2013

Toulmin, S, *The Uses of Argument*, Cambridge University Press, 1958

Vogl, J, *The Ascendancy of Finance*, Polity Press, Cambridge, 2017

Waldeman, M, *POTUS Speaks*, Simon & Schuster, New York, 2000

Watson, D, *Recollections of a Bleeding Heart*, Random House, Sydney 2002

Wills, G, *Lincoln at Gettysburg: The Words that Remade America*, Simon & Schuster, New York, 1992

Acknowledgements

THESE REFLECTIONS ON SPEECHWRITING have been a long time in the making, and if I were to acknowledge all those who helped me directly and indirectly along the years, well, it would take a small pamphlet. So I confine myself to thanking those who have been essential to my writing and my life in the creation of this book, for the reasons they know: Gabrielle Carey, Vicki Hastrich, Charlotte Wood, Tegan Bennett Daylight, Syd Hickman, Justin Holdforth, Elicia Murray, Rachel Thompson, Sally Hone, Maisie Fieschi, Jane Novak, Mary Rennie and Belinda Yuille.

Index